# THE
# SPITFIRE SUMMER

The people's-eye view of
the Battle of Britain

5

OSLO ✠

NORWAY

SWEDEN

Stavanger ✠

NORTH SEA

DENMARK

Esbjerg ✠

POLAND

Haarlem ✠

BERLIN ●

Rotterdam ✠

HOLLAND

2

GERMANY

● BRUSSELS

✠ Cologne

BELGIUM

CZECHOSLOVAKIA

LUXEMBOURG

Legend

| 2 | 3 | 5 | Luftwaffe Groups |

**10–13 GROUPS:** Fighter Command areas

AUSTRIA

# THE SPITFIRE SUMMER

The people's-eye view of
the Battle of Britain

by Peter Haining

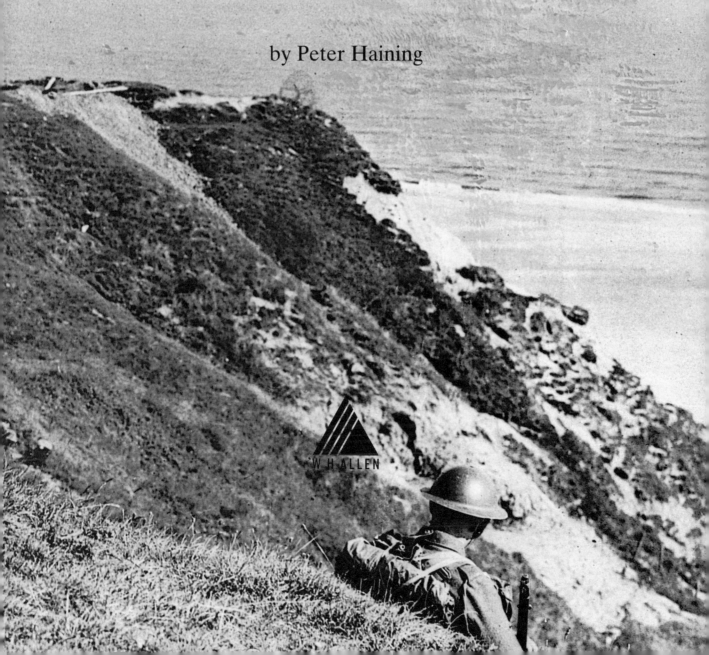

W H ALLEN

© Peter Haining 1990

First published in 1990 by W.H. Allen & Co Plc

Design: Cecil Smith

Typeset by Phoenix Photosetting
Printed and bound in Great Britain by
Butler & Tanner Ltd, Frome and London
for the publishers W.H. Allen & Co Plc,
Sekforde House, 175/9 St John Street, London EC1V 4LL

British Library Cataloguing in Publication Data

Haining, Peter 1940—
    Spitfire Summer: the people's-eye view of the Battle
of Britain.
    1. World War 2. Battle of Britain.
    I. Title
    940.54'21

ISBN 1-85227-086-1

# CONTENTS

For
Mike Hill
flying enthusiast and companion in the air

'Be great in act, as you have been in thought;
Be stirring as the time; be sure with fire;
Threaten the threatener, and outface the brow
Of bragging horror'

William Shakespeare
*King John*

'They were wonderful, weird, exciting days. Days
when aircraft left beautiful curving vapour trails in
the sky, days when some of our friends took off
and never came back, when others came back
maimed and burnt, never to fight again. Days
when the Germans at their bases back in France
must have sat and wondered, when their High
Command must have been appalled at their
growing losses, until at long last into the bullying
German mind there came the realisation that they
had lost their first battle – the Battle of Britain.'

Anonymous RAF squadron leader
Autumn 1940

# INTRODUCTION

According to numerous reports, particularly those from official sources, the Battle of Britain was fought far up in the skies above the nation, almost completely unseen by the men and women on the ground whose future it was to decide. For instance, the very first history of the conflict, *The Battle of Britain*, which was published as a booklet by HMSO in 1941 and became an immediate best-seller, states unequivocally: 'While this great battle was being fought day after day, the men and women of this country went about their business with very little idea of what was happening high above their heads in the fields of air. This battle was not shrouded in the majestic and terrible smoke of a land bombardment with its roars of guns, its flash of shells, its fountains of erupting earth. There was no sound nor fury – only a pattern of white vapour trails leisurely changing form and shape, traced by a number of tiny specks 'scintillating like diamonds in the splendid sunlight.'

While it has to be said that this account was written when the conflict was barely over and the Second World War was still very much in progress, it none the less helped create an enduring impression that the Battle of Britain was seen and experienced *only* by those directly involved in it – namely the pilots and their leaders in Fighter Command who first blunted and then turned back the might of the German Luftwaffe. There have been dozens of books about the battle, stories both of individual pilots and of the conflict as a whole, and virtually all concur with the statement made by Basil Collier in his highly regarded work *The Battle of Britain* (1962) in which he states, 'For the man in the street to follow the progress of the Battle of Britain while it was being fought was, in fact, impossible.'

*Resolute British families like this one living in a London flat waited and watched for the German onslaught in the summer of 1940.*

The use of the word 'impossible' in this context has always bothered me. It is just a little *too* definite for my liking. For though only a child when the great battle of 'the few against the many' was fought, it has always seemed to me that so vital were the events taking place that not only would the men and women of Britain surely have been very interested in what was happening, but by the very fact that aeroplanes in battle fly at all heights – often very close to the ground – there must also have been plenty to *see*. Talking to friends, relatives and, later, those directly involved – not least my own father who served with the RAF – my feelings have grown into a conviction. The people on the ground in England, particularly in the south-east where the battle raged most fiercely, *did* see a great deal and what they saw and experienced forms the basis of the pages that follow.

Herein the reader will find not the death-and-glory stories of the famous air aces of the Battle of Britain which have already been very fully told, but instead the accounts of unsung pilots who equally faced sudden death with courage whenever they took off. Alongside them are the everyday stories of the families who carried on their lives beneath the great drama – and were sometimes confronted by it in the most dramatic and unexpected ways.

To these personal experiences have been added reports from the newspapers of the day which, though subject to censorship, still provided their readers with a graphic account of what was happening. Because of the restrictions, many of the people and locations mentioned in the press were not named, but where possible I have tracked down those involved and added their names to the stories they gave anonymously at the time. Where such unmasking has proved impossible, I have still included the stories for their intrinsic merit. For what particularly impressed me about many of the accounts I have used is the fact that they were expressed in the heat of the moment when the events they described were still fresh in people's minds, and have not been influenced or even revised in the light of subsequent events. In fact, I have found myself just as moved by some of the accounts of the ordinary people as those of the great figures of the war – sometimes even more so.

Described in its simplest terms, the Battle of Britain was fought over approximately twelve weeks by about 1500 airmen who took on and held at bay the mighty Luftwaffe who were expecting to crush them and invade England in the summer of 1940. Though the dates of the Battle are subject to much debate, I have chosen to cover a crucial two-month period, from 14 July when a BBC radio broadcast first brought the sound and fury of aircraft scrapping over the English Channel into every living room, to 15 September, the famous 'Battle of Britain Day' when the German attempt to *blitzkrieg* London into ruins was thwarted by Fighter Command and the course of the war irrevocably changed.

The statistics of the war make less glamorous reading than the heroics, but should perhaps just be noted. In the United Kingdom the German raiders destroyed 457,000 houses and damaged 4,073,000, leaving the nation with a total bill for £1,297,478,656. In all – and discounting the members of the armed services – 92,873 British civilians were killed and 127,015 injured. As a matter of interest, the worst casualties did not actually occur during the period of the Battle of Britain, but on the night of 10–11 May 1941 when 1436 people were killed in London and 1792 were injured.

What follows, then, is the story of those two summer months in 1940 – the 'Spitfire Summer' – how it was lived and how it was survived, not only by the pilots of the RAF but also the ordinary men and women who, happily in large numbers, are still with us today as both parents and grandparents to mark its fiftieth anniversary. For we should never forget that it was also their victory, as well as that of 'The Few'.

Peter Haining
April 1989

*'The Battle Begins' – a dramatic picture by C.E. Turner from the* Illustrated London News, *29 June 1940.*

# THE ILLUSTRATED LONDON NEWS.

The World Copyright of all the Editorial Matter, both Illustrations and Letterpress, is Strictly Reserved in Great Britain, the British Dominions and Colonies, Europe, and the United States of America.

## SATURDAY, JUNE 29, 1940.

"THE BATTLE OF BRITAIN" BEGINS WITH LITTLE BUT LOSS TO THE GERMANS: ONE OF THE SEVEN ENEMY BOMBERS BROUGHT DOWN IN THE FIRST MASS RAID CRASHES IN ESSEX.

# 1

# THE BATTLE AT 'HELLFIRE CORNER'

For the great majority of people living in the beleaguered British Isles, what became known as the 'Battle of Britain' began with an early evening radio transmission at the end of a warm summer Sunday on 14 July 1940. Although in previous weeks there had been reports in the newspapers of occasional raids by German bombers and scattered battles between RAF and Luftwaffe fighter planes, it was this broadcast recorded 'live' at the famous White Cliffs of Dover which, at a stroke, virtually ended the 'phoney war' that had existed in the country since the declaration of war against Nazi Germany all those months ago on another Sunday, 3 September 1939. To every one who sat around their wireless receivers that July evening it brought the war with Hitler dramatically into their homes and signalled the start of what was to prove arguably the most crucial phase of the Second World War. The broadcast also somehow encapsulated all the elements of courage, bravery and skill which five years later would lead to victory for the Allies against the evil of the Axis powers.

Curiously, though, this remarkable broadcast had come about more by chance than design. During the previous week, small groups of German fighter aircraft had been making lightning strikes over the English Channel against the British shipping which was bringing much-needed supplies to the island – now standing alone against the triumphant might of the Nazi forces who had swept across Europe and were waiting on the coast of France poised for invasion. In time, their forays and the

almost maniacal fervour of those who opposed them were to earn this stretch of water off the Kent coast the nickname 'Hellfire Corner'.

That Sunday afternoon, Charles Gardner, one of the BBC's reporters who himself had not long returned across the Channel from Dunkirk following the débâcle of the fall of France in early June, was despatched with a recording van to the cliffs of Dover to give an eye-witness account of the progress of shipping in the narrow straits. Gardner was a man who had already seen the extraordinary bravery of the British pilots providing cover for the evacuation of the massed forces from France, but could have had no idea that he was to be one of the first witnesses of the next vital stage in the war. Hardly, in fact, had he and his engineer set up the microphone into which he planned to give his observations on the convoy steaming a mile or so away up the Channel than the dark grey shapes of an attacking formation of German aircraft cut across the clear blue sky. Almost at once, too, a gaggle of English fighters roared overhead from the mainland to take up the challenge.

In a voice that rose and fell with a mixture of emotion and astonishment – and against a background of screaming engines and exploding bombs – Charles Gardner made broadcasting history, relaying to the nation an on-the-spot account of what was later to be noted as one of the first of the significant battles for Britain.

'Well, now,' he began in a voice that was almost hesitant, 'the Germans are dive-bombing a convoy out at sea. There are one, two, three, four, five, six, seven German dive bombers, Junkers 87s. There's one going down on its target now. A bomb! No! – There, he's missed the ship! He hasn't hit a single ship. There are about ten ships in the convoy but he hasn't hit a single one and . . .'

Now the pitch of Charles Gardner's voice began to rise as his eyes swept the sky. 'But the British fighters are

*A pall of black smoke hangs over Dover during a German air raid on the port in July 1940. This photograph by F.G. Kirby of the* News Chronicle *was actually banned from publication at the time by the Censor.*

" *Nearly eight months this war's been on—and what have we got to show for it?* "

coming up. Here they come! The Germans are coming in an absolute steep dive, and you can see their bombs actually leave the machines and come into the water. You can hear our anti-aircraft guns going like anything. I am looking round now. I can hear machine-gun fire, but I can't see our Spitfires. They must be somewhere there. Oh, here's a plane coming down . . .'

For a moment Gardner paused, and then his tone turned to one of elation. 'Somebody's hit a German and he's coming down with a long streak – coming down completely out of control – and now a man's baled out by parachute. It's a Junkers 87 and he's going slap into the sea. There he goes – *smash!* A terrific column of water!

'Now, then – oh, there's a terrific mix-up over the Channel! It's impossible to tell which are our machines and which are German. There's a fight going on, and you

*A typical* Punch *comment on the 'phoney war', from the issue of 1 May 1940.*

*'How to Spot the German Invaders' – an instructional cut-out-and-keep page from* The Sunday Dispatch, *23 June 1940.*

Sunday Dispatch, JUNE 23. 1940.   11

# A "Sunday Dispatch" Page To Help Everyone Defend The Country

THE War Office has issued these diagram pictures of enemy troop-carrying 'planes. They are intended to guide Local Defence Volunteers and all members of the public.

Some of these pictures have been published elsewhere in the past few days, but this page contains many more details and also silhouettes of comparable British bombers. It is the only complete chart. Cut it out and hang it on your wall.

If you see an aeroplane that resembles an enemy, tell the police, an air raid warden, or the L.D.V. at once.

Here are some simple points to remember :

If the 'plane has more than two engines it is *probably* a German.

The 3-engined Junkers Ju 52 has one engine in the nose, looking like the head of a fly. These have been the 'planes most used for parachutists.

The Junkers Ju 90 has wings that sweep backwards like a swallow in flight.

Note the square-cut edges of the wings and tails of the Junkers 'planes.

If a bomber is flying low in daylight, note the colour.

British bombers are mostly painted black on the underside. (There are some silver or light green.)

The badge painted on British 'planes is like a red, white, and blue target, with the red as the bull's-eye.

German bombers are painted light blue-grey under the fuselage and wings.

Their badge is a black cross, outlined with a white band. The white band itself is outlined in black.

A black swastika is usually carried on the tail of the 'plane.

## THESE ARE THE TYPES OF GERMAN AIRCRAFT YOU ARE MOST LIKELY TO SEE

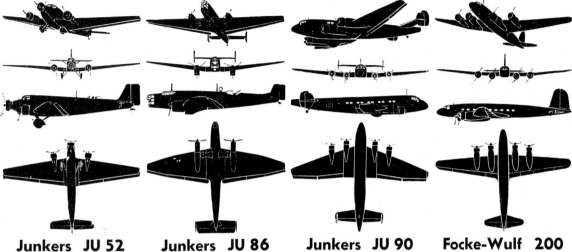

### Junkers JU 52

The Junkers 52 is the most important troop carrier and the one normally used by the Germans for parachute troops. It has a wing span of 96 feet and a length of 62 feet. Its distinctive features are :
1. Three engines.
2. Low wing.
3. Single square-cut rudder.
4. Sharply tapered wings.
5. Square-cut wing tips and tail plane.
6. Fixed undercarriage.

### Junkers JU 86

Distinctive features of the Junkers 86, which has a wing span of 73ft. 8in. and a length of 57ft. 4in., are :
1. Two engines.
2. Low wing.
3. Two square-cut rudders.
4. Sharply tapered wings.
5. Square-cut wing tips and tail plane.
6. Retractable undercarriage.

### Junkers JU 90

The Junkers JU 90, the biggest of the Junkers bombers, has a wing span of 115ft. and is 86ft. long. Its distinctive features are :
1. Four engines.
2. Low wing.
3. Two rudders.
4. Tapered wings.
5. Leading edge of wing has very pronounced "sweep back."
6. Square-cut wing tips and tail plane.
7. Retractable undercarriage.

### Focke-Wulf 200

The Focke-Wulf 200 Condor has a wing span of 108 feet and is 78 feet long. Its principal features are :
1. Four engines.
2. Low wing.
3. Single rudder.
4. Tapered wing.
5. Rounded wing tips and tail plane.
6. Retractable undercarriage.
7. Smooth stream-lined fuselage.

## BUT DON'T MISTAKE THEM FOR THESE BRITISH BOMBERS

### Whitley IV

Twin-engined long-range bomber. Undercarriage retracts. Rectangular fuselage, slightly tapered wings. Twin fins and rudders. Wing span, 84ft. 0in. ; length, 69ft. 3in.

### Hampden

Twin-engined Handley Page Hampden long-range bomber. Undercarriage retracts. Deep, narrow, rectangular fuselage with rounded transparent nose. Twin fins and rudders. Highly tapered wings. Wing span 69ft. 2in. ; length, 53ft. 7in.

### Lockheed Hudson B-14

Twin-engined bomber. Undercarriage retracts. Deep, short fuselage with twin fins and rudders and cantilever tailplane. Highly tapered wings with pointed tips. Wing span, 65ft. 6in. ; length, 44ft. 2½in.

 Cut Out This "Sunday Dispatch" Page And Pin It On The Wall At Home Or At Your Office

### Blenheim

Twin-engined Bristol Blenheim Mk. I long-range fighter and high-speed bomber. Retracting undercarriage. Fixed tail wheel. Short transparent nose, straight tapered wings with pointed tips, deep motor nacelles, bisected by wings. Single fin and rudder. Wing span 56ft. 4in. ; length 39ft. 9in.

### Wellington
Twin-engined Wellington Mk. IA long-range bomber. Power-operated turret in nose with two guns. Similar turret in tail. Undercarriage retracts backwards. Deep, well-streamlined fuselage. Highly tapered wings. Tall single fin and rudder and cantilever tailplane. Wing span, 86ft. 1in. ; length, 61ft. 3in.

| MEMORISE THIS |
| --- |
| Engines three or engines four ? There's a Nazi at the door ! |
| If the fly's head comes in view Maybe paratroopers too. |
| If the wings as swallow's lie " Still a Nazi " is the cry. |
| And among the other things Nazis like the square-clipped wings. |
| Britain's 'planes have underpart. Black as any Nazi heart. |

## HOW TO SPOT PARATROOPS

Note that paratroops drop in close formation and in larger numbers than the ordinary crew of an aeroplane. Over their uniforms they wear grey gabardine overalls. The front has a zip fastener.

Troop-dropping parachutes—this is one—are larger than normal. There is no "pilot" parachute, and the canopy is scalloped. They can drop from 300 feet.

BADGE OF PARACHUTIST AFTER SIX DESCENTS — HELMET WITH WINGED BADGE — TWO CHIN STRAPS — ROLLED CAPE — BINOCULARS — HAVERSACKS — PISTOL — WATERBOTTLE — BOMB POCKETS — BOOTS LACED AT SIDES — TUNIC COLLAR BADGE

The equipment carried by parachute troops.

'The Battle at "Hellfire Corner"' – this evocative
painting by C.E. Turner was inspired by Charles
Gardner's famous broadcast.

can hear the little rattle of machine-gun bullets. [*Crump!*] That was a bomb, as you may imagine. Here comes one Spitfire. There's a little burst. There's another bomb dropping – it has missed the convoy again. . . . You know, they haven't hit the convoy in all this. The sky is absolutely patterned with bursts of fire and the sea is covered with smoke where the bombs have hit . . .'

The words tumble from the excited reporter's lips as he sees aircraft twisting and turning in the skies above him. A few moments later and he is reporting that the German planes, perhaps as many as twenty-five of them, seem to have finished their attack and are haring back to France. Peering hard at the sky, Gardner momentarily thinks he can see two more parachutists, but then decides they must be seagulls!

'Well, that was a really hot little engagement while it lasted,' he says at last, his voice having regained its customary deliberate tone. 'No damage done, except to the Germans who lost one machine and the German pilot, who is still on the end of his parachute, though appreciably nearer the sea than he was. I can see no boat going out to pick him up, so he'll probably have a long swim ashore.'

An eerie silence falls over the air waves, and then Gardner's experienced eye spots more drama. By now, too, other people have begun to gather on the cliffs and form an excited crowd watching the battle unfolding above them.

'Oh, there's another fight going on, away up, about twenty-five or even thirty thousand feet above our heads.

Oh, we have just hit a Messerschmitt! Oh, that was beautiful! He's coming right down. . . . You hear those crowds? He's finished. Oh, he's coming down like a rocket now. An absolutely steep dive. Let us move round so we can watch him a bit more. . . . No, no, the pilot's not getting out of that one. I don't think we shall actually see him crash, because he's going into a bank of cloud. He's smoking now. I can see smoke, although we cannot count that a definite victory because I did not see him crash. He's gone behind a hill. He certainly looked out of control.'

In the minutes that followed, Gardner continued to try to make sense of what was happening to the aircraft twisting and turning high above him. In rapid succession he described a Messerschmitt weaving and diving to avoid anti-aircraft fire from the ground, then followed another German with a Spitfire hot on his tail. But he soon had to admit that it was impossible to watch the fights very clearly for long; for no sooner had one seen the twirling machines, and the bursts of machine-gun fire had reached you, he explained, than the planes were gone. There was, though, one further moment of high tension to grab his interest.

'Hello,' Gardner said as if suddenly wondering whether anyone was still listening, 'look, there's a dog-fight going on up there. There are four, five, six machines

*These three dramatic frames are from some rare film footage shot at 'Hellfire Corner' in July 1940.*

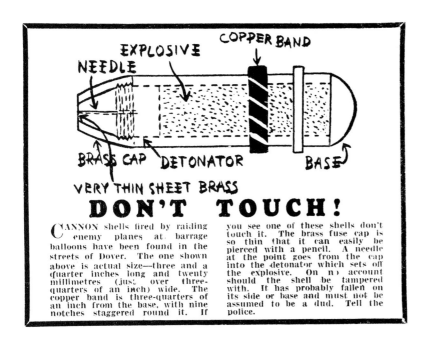

**DON'T TOUCH!**

CANNON shells fired by raiding enemy planes at barrage balloons have been found in the streets of Dover. The one shown above is actual size—three and a quarter inches long and twenty millimetres (just over three-quarters of an inch) wide. The copper band is three-quarters of an inch from the base, with nine notches staggered round it. If you see one of these shells don't touch it. The brass fuse cap is so thin that it can easily be pierced with a pencil. A needle at the point goes from the cap into the detonator which sets off the explosive. On no account should the shell be tampered with. It has probably fallen on its side or base and must not be assumed to be a dud. Tell the police.

---

# The Daily Telegraph
### and Morning Post

No. 26,555  LONDON, MONDAY, JULY 15, 1940  BROADCASTING—Page Three  ONE PENNY

## MR. CHURCHILL AND AN INVASION

### READY, UNDISMAYED, TO MEET IT

### "WE SEEK NO TERMS & ASK NO MERCY"

### LONDON IN RUINS BETTER THAN ENSLAVEMENT

Mr. Churchill, in a broadcast to British, Empire and American listeners last night, reaffirmed his confidence in the determination and ability of this country to resist invasion and, when the time comes, to lift the dark curse of Hitler from our age. He declared:

"Be the ordeal sharp or long, or both, we shall seek no terms, we shall tolerate no parley. We may show mercy, but we shall ask none."

Never before had Britain had an army comparable in quality, equipment or numbers with to-day's. London itself, fought street by street, could easily devour an entire hostile army, and we would rather see London laid in ruins and ashes than that it should be abjectly enslaved.

Looking to the future, Mr. Churchill declared that we must prepare not only for 1941, but for 1942, "when the war will, I trust, take a different form from the defensive in which it has hitherto been bound."

The Prime Minister said that in a week the Royal Air Force and Fighter Command had shot down more than five to one of the German aircraft which tried to attack convoys in the Channel.

#### FRANCE WILL BE LIBERATED

Mr. Churchill began his broadcast with a reference to the painful task which Britain now cut off from captive France of...

### U.S. DEMOCRATS MEET TO-DAY

#### THIRD TERM TAKEN FOR GRANTED

From Our SPECIAL CORRESPONDENT

CHICAGO, Sunday.

Delegates to the Democratic National Convention, which gets off to a slow-motion start to-morrow, have gathered here with three views uppermost in their minds.

The first is that it would be a grave mistake to under-estimate the strength of the Republican candidate, Mr. Wendell Willkie. The second, arising from this, is that Mr. Roosevelt must be nominated for a third term, while the third is that Mr. James Farley, Postmaster-General, must manage the campaign.

Mr. Farley has been national chairman since Mr. Roosevelt's first nomination eight years ago. He still holds himself remote from the New Dealers, headed by Mr. Harry Hopkins, Secretary for Commerce, who is now here running the Roosevelt candidacy.

Mr. Farley's opposition to a third term has been frequently expressed in the past, and he has also objected to interference by New Dealers in his domain of party organisation and strategy.

The President's acceptance of nomination is now taken for granted by a majority of Democrats.

#### NAMES ON THURSDAY

The actual work of the Convention could be concluded in two days. But delegates must be given an opportunity to spend money for the benefit of the city of Chicago; so the Presidential nominations will not take place until Thursday.

The names of Mr. Farley and Mr. Garner, Vice-President, will, according to present plans, be offered as well as Mr. Roosevelt's. The Vice-Presidential candidate presents some difficulty. Mr. Roosevelt may solve the problem by asking Mr. Garner to run again, although he has organised opposition in the Senate to many of the President's policies.

#### LUXURY TAX EXPECTED

NEW BUDGET PLANS

By Our Political Correspondent

Sir Kingsley Wood, Chancellor of the Exchequer, may make an announcement in the House of Commons this week on the future of the Purchase Tax Bill and the...

FRENCH NATIONAL DAY IN LONDON

Gen. de Gaulle inspecting a French guard of honour in Whitehall before he placed a wreath on the Cenotaph in celebration of the French national holiday yesterday—the anniversary of the fall of the Bastille. Adml. Muselier is on the left. (Another picture on Page 6.)

### EIRE WARNED BY MINISTER

#### May Soon Be In A Tight Corner

WAR-TIME ADVICE TO PEOPLE

FROM OUR OWN CORRESPONDENT

DUBLIN, Sunday.

Mr. F. Aiken, Minister for Co-ordination of Defence, in Eire, speaking at a recruiting meeting in Dundalk to-day, said: "We may be in a rather tight corner soon, but that is nothing new to us, and with God's help and the courage of our people we will pull this old land through."

He added that every civilian must realise that his district might become the scene of military operations at any time. In such a case, they should observe the following points:—

Do not hinder the Army by crowding the roads or do anything which hampers the Army's operations against the enemy.

Do not co-operate with or assist the enemy in any way.

Obey all instructions issued by the Army, police, local security forces and A.R.P. services.

Learn first aid to protect yourself...

## 60-MINUTE AIR BATTLE OFF DOVER

### 7 NAZIS DOWN : DIRECT A.A. HIT

Pilots of the R.A.F. Fighter Command and anti-aircraft gunners yesterday combined to shoot down seven enemy aircraft in air fights off the South-East Coast. Other enemy 'planes were hit and may also have been destroyed.

About 40 Ju. 87 dive bombers were engaged as well as a number of escorting Me. 109 fighters.

The anti-aircraft guns were firing almost continuously for more than half an hour. In the air the fight continued for a full hour, many of the Junkers being chased back across the English Channel.

This latest success, which follows those of last week, when 84 German bombers and fighters...

### R.A.F. STRIKE AT RAID BASES

## BRITISH ATTACK AFTER FOUR-DAY SIEGE

### ADVANCE OVER RIVER BED AGAINST ITALIANS

From Our Special Correspondent, ALEXANDER CLIFFORD

CAIRO, Sunday.

Deep in the heart of Africa a little British garrison is holding out heroically against a spectacular Italian offensive.

This is at British Moyale, on the Kenya-Abyssinia border, where the defenders are repulsing attacks on a scale out of all proportion to the place's value. The garrison has been holding out for four days and heavy fighting continues.

In the western desert, whence I have just returned, I learned how the difficulties of Marshal Graziani, the Italian Commander-in-Chief in Libya, caused this Kenya outpost to be his No. 1 objective.

### PEACE MOVE IN FAR EAST

#### BRITISH EFFORT AT MEDIATION

SINGAPORE, Sunday.

Efforts by the British Government to bring peace between China and Japan were disclosed in a broadcast to-night by Mr. S. W. Jones, Acting Governor of Malaya.

At the moment, he stated, the British Government was discussing with the Japanese Government certain proposals affecting the war which the latter had advanced.

"Believing that an honourable peace is the real desire of the Chinese and Japanese peoples," he continued, "his Majesty's Government will go to the greatest length to avoid seconding and prolonging the war in the East and will put forward every effort it can afford to end it. What the result will be we shall soon know."

In the long battle she was fighting against heavy odds Britain was forced to summon up every effort and make every sacrifice to gain a victory against Germany, which was the sole hope of civilisation.

It had been one of her saddest trials to see China and Japan, formerly allies of the Empire, locked in mortal combat, and it had been the earnest hope of the British...

He has ordered artillery fire of great intensity, while bombers and fighters have been trying to flatten out the British defences and pave the way for the final capture.

But the undaunted defenders are not giving up their positions yet. They have even launched a number of counter-attacks against the Italians entrenched in their own fort.

Our 'planes have been finding excellent targets in the Italian convoys, which are continually bringing up supplies of ammunition and reinforcements to enable the attack to continue. Even if the Italians occupy the British positions they will find themselves in another Fort Capuzzo with the surrounding countryside controlled by deadly British patrols.

#### CHEAP SUCCESS SOUGHT

This offensive is a sequel to the message, which Graziani is reported to have received from Rome after Marshal Balbo's death. Angered at the news that British patrols were in possession of an area of Libya larger than Yorkshire, Mussolini decided to carry the war into Egypt and gain a cheap success by the capture of Sollum.

Accordingly Italian propaganda started to build up this miserable collection of whitewashed cottages, which has a...

---

*The German Air Force on the doorstep of England – a front page report in the* Daily Telegraph *of 15 July.*

whirling and turning around. Now – hark at those machine guns going – there's something coming right down on the tail of another. Here they come. Yes, they are being chased home! There are three Spitfires chasing three Messerschmitts now. Oh, boy! Look at them going! There is a Spitfire behind the first two. He will get them. Oh, yes. I've never seen anything so good as this. The RAF fighters have really got these boys taped. Our machine is catching up the Messerschmitt now. He's got the legs of it, you know. Now right in the sights. Go on, George! You've got him! Bomb – bomb! No, no, the distance is a bit deceptive from here. You can't tell, but I think something definitely is going to happen to that first Messerschmitt. I wouldn't like to be him.'

Almost out of breath, Gardner paused once again. The other onlookers on the cliffs seemed to draw closer to him as he went on making history – adding their eyes to his own. He continued: 'I think he's got him. Yes? Oh, look. Where? Where? I can't see them at all. Just on the left of those black spots. See it? Oh, yes, oh yes, I see it. Yes, they've got him down. Yes, the Spitfire has pulled away from him. Yes, I think that first Messerschmitt has crashed on the coast of France all right.'

Charles Gardner was literally out of breath as the battle at 'Hellfire Corner' drew to its victorious close. He was scarcely aware of the radio engineer packing away the equipment – having first carefully checked that the precious recording was safe – nor of climbing into the van for the return journey to London. Indeed, when the report was broadcast just over four hours later – in full and completely unedited – Gardner had the uncanny feeling he was listening to someone else talking, so drained had he been by the experience.

Radio listeners across the nation heard Gardner's eye-witness account in stunned silence. No one, except those servicemen who had flown in direct contact with

*The invaders are on the doorstep: an ME 109 that failed to make it back to France and was shot down on the south coast of England.*

**Some Lines by a Sergeant Pilot**

God, give us grace that we,
Flying our fighters to eternity,
May meteor-like before we fall
Leave fiery trails of light, that all
Truth's sons may clutch, and clutching rise,
To blast Hell's spawn from Heaven's skies.

*(Punch, 3 July 1940)*

the enemy, had ever been this close to the action before. As one commentator wrote later, 'The Gardner broadcast caused a sensation, and was a modern war innovation as remarkable as the advent of the aeroplane itself.'

Undoubtedly, the transmission was full of the ardour of a young man with an instinctive love for flying and the RAF, and his emotion was as moving as it was graphic. Today, fifty years on, the record of that momentous moment in history, carefully preserved in the BBC archives, is still capable of catching the throat of anyone who listens to it.

Yet, this said, the fact remains that *not* everyone was impressed by the broadcast. Indeed, in the next few days Charles Gardner's account generated a controversy that raged through the pages of the national press and on the radio itself. For while there were clearly millions of men and women who had been enthralled and inspired by the report, there were others who believed that a battle of life and death was not a fit subject for broadcasting.

One of the first to object was a man who had himself flown as a pilot in the First World War. Now a member of the clergy, the Reverend R.H. Hawkins from Dalston in Carlisle wrote to *The Times* in the immediate aftermath.

'Will you allow me to record my protest against the eye-witness account of the air fight over the Straits of Dover given by the BBC *News* on Sunday evening? Some of the details were bad enough; but far more revolting was the spirit in which these details were given to the public. Where men's lives are concerned, must we be treated to a running commentary on a level with an account of the Grand National or a Cup Final tie? Does the BBC imagine that the spirit of the nation is to be fortified by gloating over the grimmer details of fighting?'

Clearly there were those who thought the nation *would* be fortified: a Londoner, Charles Fisher, replied almost by return.

'I also listened to the broadcast, but my reactions were very different from those of the Reverend R.H. Hawkins. It was something quite different from 'an account of the Grand National or Cup Final'; to me it was inspiring, for I almost felt I was sharing in it, and I rejoiced unfeignedly that so many of the enemy were shot down, and the rest were put to ignominious flight. My uplift of heart was due to a better understanding, which the BBC enabled me to get, of the courage and daring of our pilots, and the reality and nature of the

*A Spitfire pilot prepares to go on patrol over the skies of southern England.*

victory they are achieving for us. We are proud of their feats, and such a description as Mr Gardner gave made it possible for us to rejoice with them. I fancy his commentary caught something of the spirit of the pilots themselves.'

The debate as to the virtues of the broadcast spread from newspaper to newspaper, those in favour of the transmission far outweighing those who objected. But there were those – possibly wishing to bury their heads in the sand – who felt it had brought the conflict uncomfortably close to home; while others of perhaps an even more unrealistic nature believed it to have been an exercise in bloodthirsty propaganda. What *is* unquestioned about the report is the light that it sheds for us today on a nation quite unused to eye-witness accounts of death – now, of course, very much an everyday part of our lives courtesy of television.

In time, the BBC itself felt compelled to comment on the furore that the broadcast had raised, and the following statement was issued from Broadcasting House by F.W. Ogilvie, an assistant to the Director General.

'People in all walks of life have assured us since this broadcast that they found it heartening and a tonic. One group of fifteen listeners voted it "the finest thing the BBC has ever done". Many have suggested that a record should be sold for the Red Cross. Others have hoped that it would be relayed to America [as, in fact, it was], to show the British spirit at this moment. These comments came from all parts of the island. On the other side there were objectors, though not many.'

Mr Ogilvie then briefly restated the principles by which the BBC proposed to guide itself through the coming conflict. 'Broadcasting must face the war as do individuals in and out of uniform,' he said. 'There is a debatable borderline between gaiety and levity, between the cheapness and the cheerfulness that springs from a stout heart. Evidently I shall not persuade some of our critics that we are not guilty of crossing to the wrong side with our broadcast. Other critics, no less detached and reputable, believe us to have been right. Listeners as a body will, we hope and believe, give us the credit for being aware of that borderline and, equally, of having no intention of being browbeaten into the safe regions of the colourless.'

With hindsight, it seems evident to me that Charles Gardner's broadcast that Sunday night not only brought the sound and fury of battle into the nation's living rooms for the first time, but equally helped to concentrate the people's thoughts on just *how* close the enemy was. It provided a unique clarion call to the country, which had not had a potential invader close to its shores since William the Conqueror prepared to cross almost nine hundred years before.

## THE SMELL OF WAR

HERE at Dover, on the heights from which you can see the enemy's gun flashes and the dim outline of his coast, there's a sort of invisible vapour about which smells of war. It's all-pervading. It's almost as if one could catch a breath of the putrefaction which the Nazi has spread over Europe. Yes – you have got to come to the very edge of the island to realise adequately the threat of invasion. It would seem sometimes that it is easy to forget it. Easy to imagine the danger past because the worst hasn't yet happened – that is the deadly error of Norway and Holland and Belgium. At this very moment, when curious political diversions are taking place – at this moment when the Hun is taking soundings about a so-called New Order in Continental Europe – this is the time when the cobra may strike.

Here there is a full awareness of it. Here, along

these cliffs, so completely characteristic of England. I have come back to the Old Country from foreign parts through most of her gateways. None is so heart-lifting to the returned exile as this harbour I know so well, with the English green above the white chalk. And I must say I like chalk. Clean, homely, pleasant, malleable stuff, with so many uses. You can improve your billiards with it, or paint your hen-house with it, or bore tunnels in it to defy the bomber. Tunnels – I think I have walked through miles of these endless chalk galleries opening into vaulted store rooms, and even into beautifully organised dressing stations and operation rooms. All things in Dover start from chalk.

I have just been over the defences here, down the sloping planes of the cliffs to the water's edge, and along the coast to Romney Marsh. The famous sheep in those wet flats must by this time be

*Official War Ministry photographs of the British defences against invasion.*

thoroughly broken-in to the sound of crashing Junkers and Messerschmitts. Well, I walked gingerly about the place and saw what there was to see – but naturally, put in most time at the batteries. Once a gunner, always a gunner. I like to watch these engaging monsters swing their questing muzzles about on the touch of a wheel, and to see the smooth play of the brass elevating and traversing gears, and the workmanlike snugness of the casemates.

Along the coastline I visited headquarters of battalions and companies that, after a period of rigorous training, were now established in the front fortified system. Ah—this is a real, good reception area down here for Nazi evacuees. No possible device for their suitable entertainment has been left out. Barbed wire and machine-gun emplacements and guns, and tank traps and more guns, and ingenious dodges of all sorts – every curve and gully of this peaceful Kentish countryside is swept and garnished for the guests: those of them, that is to say, who manage to survive the attentions of the Navy and the RAF. How different all this must have looked in May last, when the gates were almost wide open!

Thank God Britain is still an island, in spite of pre-war theorising by Continental pundits. The obscene Goebbels and his litter in Berlin can falsify the history books. But not even Nazi propaganda can monkey with geography. Yes, but there must be no stupid belief in security. Our defences are now formidable and methodical behind these ever-blessed Straits. But only a few miles away is the giant army that has smashed its way through Western Europe, an unprecedented battering-ram at the disposal of a cunning and merciless gang. There is no trick, no treachery, no murderous invention they will not use to destroy this country, which alone stands between them and the world's loot. All this means we cannot afford to slacken for a moment.

I talked to a regular sergeant at a post down here. He had been in the hottest corners of the march from Louvain to Dunkirk, and with his battalion had just come here after a period of the most intensive training he'd ever experienced. He said: 'It was tough, but we were glad of it. This show in France taught us all you had to be well-trained or nothing.' This is the true word. Any slackening in attention, in discipline, in readiness along all this coast, might mean a sudden breach in the defences. We must go on making the best, the most efficient, the most modern, the most highly trained army there is – and this should be commended to those people who seem to think that you can safely take the Army off its job.

Walking about in the streets reminds me of another thing this war has done – it has wiped out any invidious distinction between soldiers and civilians. Again, that's not at all like the last war. We really *are* all in it together this time.

Captain Alan Harper, Royal Artillery
*The Listener*, July 1940

# 2

# OUT OF THE FRYING PAN INTO THE SPITFIRE

Despite the harsh weather of January and February 1940 – two of the coldest months on record in this century – the British people approached the summer of that year with a courageous sense of optimism, regardless of the proximity of the German forces and, following the fall of France, an almost overwhelming sense of isolation. It was, in fact, that indefinable quality known as the 'British Spirit' which was enabling men, women and children to go resolutely about their daily lives in as normal a fashion as possible, despite evacuation, rationing, blackout and the ever-present threat of German air raids; that 'British Spirit' – plus the trait of mild eccentricity and lively sense of humour that unites the people and in times of adversity enables them to smile through everything.

Today, looking at the self-same newspapers that dropped through the nation's front doors each morning that July (with the same regularity as the milkmen calling and the postmen bringing welcome mail, bombs notwithstanding) and which informed the British people of the progress of the war, these eight-page papers help to paint a vivid picture of life in the beleaguered nation. For despite columns of news about the war abroad and large numbers of official bulletins from government sources urging citizens to be economical in their use of food, careful about concealing lights in their homes after dark,

and to hold their tongues, there are plenty of other signs of life going on very much as usual. The advertisements, too, though fewer in number, are still busy promoting products such as Kellogg's Corn Flakes, Persil Washing Powder, Guinness, Player's cigarettes and Cadbury's chocolate (not forgetting Rennies for indigestion, and Bile Beans 'To keep you Young & Attractive'!) – though in many cases opportunist copywriters took full advantage of the uncertain times to accentuate the value of their goods. Bovril, for example, raised its lid to the splendid women of Britain and said that a daily mug of the hot beverage would 'help them to maintain the fitness that exacting work demands'.

Outside the home, pubs and restaurants were open (though their fare was noticeably depleted), as were the dance halls, cinemas and theatres. In London, the top films that month were *Gone with the Wind*, Walt Disney's *Pinocchio*, Garbo in *Ninotchka* and, at the Stoll Theatre in Kingsway, the rather inappropriately titled *We Are Not Alone!* On the stage, *Chu Chin Chow* was playing to full houses, Lupino Lane was 'still carrying on' in *Me and My Girl*, John Gielgud was starring in *The Tempest* at the Old Vic, and Max Miller was in George Black's *Haw Haw. Come out of Your Shell*, the title of the revue at the Criterion, seemed somehow to epitomise the message the entertainment world was trying to get across. (Interestingly, too, Madame Tussaud's Exhibition was announcing a new attraction: a large, bemedalled figure of Field Marshal Goering!)

In the field of sport, golf and tennis were still being played wherever the clubs' land had not been commandeered by the forces. (The All England Tennis Club was,

*The 'British spirit' typified – posters such as this urged women to join the war effort.*

Dunlop and Bovril were just two of many companies
who utilised the war in their advertising in the summer
of 1940.

**DUNLOP TYRES** *do their Duty!*

radio on 12 July as part of their propaganda campaign, which claimed that there was a 'sports war' going on in the country against plutocratic cricketers. 'People have tried to destroy the playing grounds at night,' said the announcer, 'and this has led to a sort of state of war between the population and the English sports clubs'!

It did not, however, need the wild fantasies of the German propaganda machine to portray the English as eccentrics – they were quite capable of doing *that* for themselves! For also in the pages of the newspapers in July 1940 could be found people exercising their minds – and pens – about such diverse matters as the imposition of tea rationing, the annoyance of air-raid sirens and the fact that the cuckoo seemed to have deserted the countryside earlier than usual! This might well have been an omen that things were to change dramatically before the month was out!

It was on Tuesday 9 July that the nation's favourite beverage was finally rationed after several months of uncertainty. A shortage of beer and cigarettes since the winter had been bad enough, but now there was to be less tea! The outcry was immediate, especially from workers in factories, offices and shops where the only way of getting a cuppa was to bring in some of their own precious supplies from home. Before the end of the month, however, the Ministry of Food was forced to take action, releasing the following announcement on 24 July.

'The Ministry of Food has authorised Food Control Committees to issue special permits for the purchase of tea for industrial, business and clerical workers in cases where they cannot obtain tea from the registered canteens. This will enable them to have tea during their working hours without drawing on their domestic rations.'

A shortage of eggs was another increasing aggravation in July 1940, though the *Daily Express*'s famous columnist, 'Beachcomber', may well have defused the arguments in many a household with the following amusing report on 3 July.

'Of all the stories of economic warfare, the one that pleases me most is the story of the pickled Polish egg. The egg was photographed and examined by experts because the police had detected some writing on it. When deciphered the message turned out to be either (a) One of good will, or (b) One of ill will, towards England in an obscure Carpathian dialect. Further examination was necessary. But, alas, during one of its journeys from department to department the egg got broken.'

'Beachcomber' concluded that the message was in all probability 'one of affection scribbled by a girl packer for the eye of a young loader'!

It was in that same week that the issue of the cuckoo (and the grouse) came to the fore, the cause being the disappearance of one and the surfeit of the other. *The*

however, having some problems with the pig farm that had been started in their grounds!) Athletics, greyhound racing, horse-race meetings and cricket were continuing, too – though in the case of the latter, with fewer players to draw upon, arranging matches was something of a struggle. Sportsmen as a whole were afforded a smile by an extraordinary story broadcast in English by German

# BOVRIL "doffs the cap" to the splendid women of Britain . .

In every sort of war-time task that women can do—and in a great many that women were never expected to be able to do—the women of Britain are scoring triumph after triumph. The Services, munitions, the land, transport, hospitals, canteens, all bear witness to their skill and their courage. Bovril applauds their achievements and at the same time helps them to maintain the fitness that exacting work demands.

# HOT BOVRIL CHEERS!

*Sidney Strube's famous cartoon comment on the idea of musical air-raid sirens. Strube's little figure became very familiar during the war years and was widely regarded as representing 'Everyman'.*

*Times*' nature correspondent enquired of his readers on Monday 8 July, 'Has the cuckoo gone?' And he continued: 'There has been no sound of him here, on the southern fringe of Surrey, since June 21, and although there may be later records from other parts of the country, it looks as if he has gone much earlier than the old rhyme says he should.'

Perhaps, one joker in another paper suggested, the cuckoo had heard of the Government's intention to bring forward the grouse shooting season and feared he might get mistaken for the game bird? Though meant only in jest, the basis of this theory *was* true, as an Order in Council entitled the Defence (Game) Regulations had stipulated an opening date of 5 August rather than the 'Glorious Twelfth', because 'birds look like being plentiful this year while sportsmen and cartridges will be fewer'.

Public interest in the welfare of birds, however, was as nothing to the rising tide of protests about the wail of air-raid sirens. Mr John Simpson, of Manchester, wrote to the *News Chronicle* on the subject.

'Is there no way of impressing upon those in authority that the noise of the siren is getting more people down than anything else at present? There is nothing the German Nazi can do as far as I am concerned that can make me give in, but the noise of our sirens is doing something to me quite definitely – and doing it well! The scream of those unspeakable instruments after six hours' loss of sleep last night made me really ill – quite literally! And I know that there are thousands of others who feel as I do.'

Indeed, there were quite a number among the 'thousands' Mr Simpson spoke about who also complained to their newspapers – people such as Mr Thomas Swan of Edmonton, London, who came up with a practical alternative in the columns of the *Daily Express*. He suggested that music be used instead to

*Members of a Home Guard unit watching enemy action near Dover. A balloon exploding after being shot by a German raider.*

A Home Guard stationed near the south coast hard at work in July 1940 making molotov cocktails in case of invasion!

herald the approach and departure of German raiders!

'The sound of the siren could be replaced by the tones of "The Campbells Are Coming",' Mr Swan suggested, 'which, while conveying a definite warning, at the same time implies a hearty defiance and a certain zest for the fray. As the all-clear, I would suggest we could hardly do better than, "Who's Afraid of the Big Bad Wolf?"' (Mr Swan's letter, and others like it from fellow sufferers, inspired one of the summer's most memorable cartoons in the *Daily Express* – 'Warn Us With Music' by Straub, which is reprinted on page 30.

Initially the Ministry of Home Security, who were primarily responsible, tried to counter all the complaints with what they evidently believed to be helpful advice on how to look after the ears during raids. But in attempting to placate people they really succeeded only in exacerbating the situation by releasing statements headed 'Protection of Ears in Air Raids' which remarked, with staggering insensitivity, 'It is pointed out that noise during air raids constitutes one of the main dangers to morale. Violent noises, when they are repeated at short intervals, are apt to create a shock to the nervous system . . .'

The Ministry's advice to plug the ears with either rubber or ebonite earplugs, softened beeswax material, or cotton wool coated with Vaseline, was all very well – but obviously none of these could be worn until *after* the alert had been given. Following relentless public pressure for several weeks, *The Times* finally carried this announcement on Saturday 7 September: 'Instructions have been given by the Ministry of Home Security to reduce the period of sounding of the Air Raid Warning sirens (warbling note) from two minutes to one minute. The 'raiders past' signal (steady blast) will continue to be sounded for two minutes.' It was not much of a triumph for the protesters – and by then, of course, London was the target of the terrible German *blitzkrieg*.

The nation's Home Guard, then almost 500,000 strong, also found itself the butt of a German propaganda campaign in July 1940. This remarkable 'army' of men either too old for military service or engaged in reserved occupations had been inaugurated on 14 May of that year, and across the nation fellows of all ages could be found on village greens and in town halls training to handle weapons to repel German invaders. There were those who regarded the Home Guard with a certain wry amusement – a fact which has been splendidly portrayed in the long-running BBC TV series *Dad's Army* – but no one either then or now could surely hope to be taken seriously in describing the men

*Prime Minister Winston Churchill testing one of the new 'Tommy Guns' imported from America; and (right) the Daily Express article on 'the gangster's favourite weapon'!*

## This is a Tommy gun

TOMMY-GUNS, which proved so effective in the hands of Nazi para-troops, are now being sent to this country from the U.S. at the rate of 5,000 a month.

They weigh 12½lbs. They are two feet in length and can fire thirty rounds in four seconds. This is all their magazine's hold Tommy - guns cannot con-tinue their rate of fire as a Bren gun can, and they are only effective at fifty to seventy - five yards.

A Tommy-gun, in fact, is a short - range weapon ideal for Parashots.

MAGAZINE

# To The Women of Britain

# GIVE US YOUR ALUMINIUM

*Out of the frying pan . . . into the Spitfire.*

WE want aluminium, and we want it now.
New and old of every type and description, and all of it.

We will turn your pots and pans into Spitfires and Hurricanes, Blenheims and Wellingtons.

I ask, therefore, that everyone who has pots and pans, kettles, vacuum cleaners, hat pegs, coat hangers, shoe trees, bathroom fittings and household ornaments, cigarette boxes, or any other articles made wholly or in part of aluminium, should hand them over at once to the local headquarters of the Women's Voluntary Services.

There are branches of this organisation in every town and village in the country.

But if you are in any doubt, if you have difficulty in finding the local office of the Women's Voluntary Services, please inquire at the nearest police station or town hall, where you will be supplied with the necessary information.

The need is instant. The call is urgent. Our expectations are high.

*Beaverbrook*

as 'an armed gang of guerillas'. But that is precisely what the Bremen radio station in Germany endeavoured to do!

In tones of some gravity, the station's announcer was heard reporting: 'It is once more emphasised in Berlin official circles that the preparations which are being made all over Britain to arm the civilian population for guerilla warfare are contrary to the rules of international law. The British Government seems determined to disregard all the warnings given by Germany hitherto.'

Any Home Guard listening must have found himself shaking with mirth as the voice went on: 'Further documentary evidence has now reached Berlin indicating that the preparations now being made for armed gangs are being carried on and with the full knowledge and consent of the Government. The evidence includes photographs which have appeared in the press of the United States showing British civilians being instructed in the use of firearms of all kinds.'

In truth, there was nothing special about these photographs at all, for British papers, too, had carried pictures of enthusiastic milkmen, butchers, bus conductors, train drivers, clerks and so on busy learning to handle rifles (more often than not represented by broom handles) and arresting supposed invaders (bundles of rags or bags of hay). But if this was not proof enough that Britain was turning her civilians into a population of *francs-tireurs*, the German announcer thundered, what about the article by an 'English military expert' entitled 'Armed Citizens'?

'Besides containing detailed instructions on the use of arms,' the presenter continued, 'the article describes the digging of trenches and the preparation of tank traps and dug-outs, and states that any weapon is good enough to kill Germans with. This documentary evidence proves the state of mind prevailing in Great Britain!'

What publication, any innocent listener might have wondered, could possibly have carried such dastardly writings? None other than the *Picture Post*!

Interestingly, though the Home Guard were clearly never intended to be armed gangs, it has been revealed since the war that a school for guerilla warfare *was* organised in London in 1940 as part of last-ditch plans for defending the capital. Recruits learned how to make shotguns more deadly by loading them with ball bearings, and how to garrotte unsuspecting invaders with piano wires!

Some newspapers, too, advised readers how to be ready to protect themselves. The *Daily Express*, for example, alongside a report that the Thompson Automatic Gun Company in America was sending over the gangsters' favourite 'Tommy Guns' at the rate of 5000

*Lord Beaverbrook, the Minister of Aircraft Production, who worked a miracle creating new aircraft for Fighter Command. (left) His appeals to the women of Britain to hand over their aluminium utensils produced a tremendous response.*

per month (see report), also gave advice on how to make Molotov cocktails! The paper's famous columnist William Hickey, taking a break from reporting the doings of what remained of London's 'fashionable set', suggested that as the London defence volunteers were unarmed "they may care to have the recipe" – and then provided it in precise detail!

Surprising as it may have been to discover such a report in the pages of a national newspaper, it was perhaps less surprising in the pages of the *Daily Express* than any other for the proprietor was none other than Lord Beaverbrook, the fiery Canadian-born press

(above) *A housewife in Kingston-upon-Thames handing over a saucepan to a member of the WVS.* (right) *The result of Lord Beaverbrook's appeals was busy production lines building new Spitfires.*

baron whom Winston Churchill had just appointed as Minister of Aircraft Production. The skill, verve and tireless dedication that Beaverbrook brought to his job of readying the RAF for its battle in the skies with the Luftwaffe unquestionably made him one of the heroes of the 'Spitfire Summer'. He was determined to lead by example, and his clarion call to the hundreds of thousands of people involved in this work was dramatically direct: 'The production which you pour out of your factories this week will be hurled into the desperate struggle next week.'

A humble Canadian clergyman's son who had made a fortune as a stockbroker before coming to Britain where he entered Parliament, Beaverbrook then took over the *Daily Express* and rapidly turned it into the most widely read newspaper in the world. He was a passionate believer in the British Empire, and not surprisingly used the *Express* to promote his causes. Hitler's onslaught on all that he held dear was the spark he needed to bring out all the dynamism and administrative brilliance of his character in the cause of Britain.

Although his organisation of the aircraft industry was obviously the key factor in producing the planes needed to fight the Battle of Britain, it was for his campaign to win the support of the general public that he is best remembered. In a bold statement issued on 10 July he appealed to the people of Britain to hand over their aluminium to be used to manufacture fighters and bombers. It was a challenge directed in particular at the country's housewives.

'Give us your aluminium,' Beaverbrook appealed. 'We want it, and we want it now. New and old, of every type and description, and all of it.' The front pages of all the nation's national newspapers carried Beaverbrook's words the following morning – regardless of whether or not they were normally implacable rivals of his *Daily Express*.

'We will turn your pots and pans into Spitfires and Hurricanes, Blenheims and Wellingtons. I ask, therefore, that everyone who has pots and pans, kettles, vacuum cleaners, hat-pegs, coat-hangers, shoe trees, bathroom fittings and household ornaments, cigarette boxes, or any other articles made wholly or in part of aluminium, should hand them over at once to the local headquarters of the Women's Voluntary Services. The need is instant. The call is urgent. Our expectations are high.'

It was an appeal written with the directness that characterised Beaverbrook himself – and the response was immediate and overwhelming. So overwhelming, in fact, that vast quantities of the items handed over at local depots were to remain untouched and unneeded for the rest of the war!

In the excitement of the moment in July, however, 'Aluminium Fever' caught the imagination of the nation – as well as the leader writers of other newspapers. The *Daily Sketch*, for one, brilliantly headlined its support for the campaign with the words, 'From the Frying Pan into the Spitfire!'

Anxious not to be excluded from the appeal, not a few male readers wrote to their respective papers suggesting what contributions *they* might make. In *The Times*, for example, the secretary of the Fly-Fishers Club wrote, 'Would all fishing friends and other sportsmen please send to the Fly-Fishers Club the following articles without delay – aluminium fly boxes, rod cases, landing-net frames and gaffs; shooting sticks and aluminium boot trees.' The secretary – with the appropriate name of H.D. Gillies – said that the Piccadilly-based club had made special arrangements to receive these items and see to their immediate disposal. ('Gillie', for those who might not know, is the Scottish name for a fisherman's attendant.)

On the 'Live-Letter Box' page of the *Daily Mirror*, Mr H. Rountree of Southall in Middlesex argued that golfers could be every bit as helpful as fishermen: 'As a golfer, might I suggest that my fellow golfers should collect all their old steel-shafted clubs with iron heads to help in this scrap iron campaign? Aluminium ashtrays, of which there must be so many at countless 'nineteenth holes', would also be useful!'

A more practical idea that Beaverbrook instituted was the 'Spitfire Fund' which encouraged people to make donations towards the cost of new aircraft – with the added attraction that those who contributed enough to build an entire plane could choose its name. Curiously, the idea of the fund was developed from a request directed to the Ministry of Aircraft Production offices by a West Indian newspaper, the *Jamaican Gleaner*, enquiring about the cost of planes. When a figure of £20,000 was mentioned for a Wellington bomber, a cheque for this sum duly arrived a few days later, donated by the paper's readers.

With his instinct for a good idea, Beaverbrook seized on this and launched the Spitfire Fund, calculating the cost of the more glamorous aircraft like the Spitfires and Hurricanes at £5000 each. In the weeks and months that followed, hardly a plane rolled off the production lines that did not bear a designation revealing those who had contributed to its costs, and there was soon hardly a town in Britain or a major organisation or body of people not represented. Individual gifts of a few pence from children 'to help the pilots', ranging to thousands of pounds from sympathetic foreign countries, were also put to the same use.

Among the many fascinating donations on record from the summer of 1940 can be listed an amazing

*" All right then—loser pays for a Spitfire."*

£50,000 from the people of the Falkland Islands (the population then was just 3000); a cheque for £20,000 from the Heinz factory workers; £5000 from Kennel Club members (who wanted their Spitfire named 'The Dog Fighter'), and five shillings sent by Nelly Ford, the well-known flower seller at Victoria Station. 'I don't mind what it goes to,' she said in her accompanying letter, 'even if it is towards the cost of engraving the name Hitler on the biggest bomb that can be made.'

*A topical* Punch *comment on the 'Spitfire Fund', by the magazine's art editor Frank Reynolds, on 26 July 1940.*

The most poignant gift of all received by Lord Beaverbrook, however, was a donation from a Mrs M.E. Boothroyd of Walton, Liverpool – who, he confessed, almost brought tears to his eyes with her postal order for ten shillings. 'It represents the savings of my three-year-old son, killed recently in an air raid,' she wrote. 'I hope in this small way to help avenge my innocent baby's death.'

The aircraft industry itself responded magnificently to the show of public support. Working unbroken shifts, the figures of production rose steadily from a monthly output of 325 in May to 446 in June, and in July – what was to prove the peak month – the figure reached 496. Though the number fell to 476 in August and 467 in September, there was no denying that Beaverbrook had inspired the industry to produce 650 more fighters than had been estimated before his arrival, and that as a direct result the RAF never had less than 127 Spitfires and Hurricanes in reserve during the Battle of Britain.

Winston Churchill was quick to praise Beaver-brook's contribution. 'He has worked a miracle,' the Prime Minister told Parliament. 'The enemy still has more machines, but our production has now passed his. First we needed to gain parity, and next the superiority on which in a large measure the decision of the war depends.' Indeed, to adapt Churchill's famous phrase, never had so few pilots owed so much to so many.

The man in charge of this battle, Fighter Command's Air Chief Marshal Hugh Dowding, also later paid tribute to Beaverbrook's contribution in much the same way as his chief. 'The effect of his appointment can only be described as magical, and thereafter the supply situation improved to such a degree that the heavy aircraft wastage which occurred during the Battle of Britain ceased to be the primary danger, its place being taken by the difficulty of producing trained fighter pilots in adequate numbers.'

How the country had raised its band of 'The Few', and the crucial part Dowding played in it, form the next chapter in the story of the 'Spitfire Summer'.

*Photographs from a Home Guard's album – in this case, the author's uncle. (left) Bob Pattrick in his Home Guard uniform and (below) members of his unit guarding a crashed Heinkel HE 111.*

# The Army of the Night

## George Hicks MP, on the Home Guard

THE other evening I saw some Home Guard training. They were raw, they were awkward, some were elderly, and some—like myself—showed signs of living too sedentary a life. But they were willing, eager, and full of fighting spirit. Many were veterans of the last war. Seeing them, and knowing their toughness and indomitable courage, I thought of the warm welcome the enemy would get, should an invasion be attempted.

Britain bristles these days. It is armed and alert, and never so strangely so as at night. There is something terribly menacing, mysteriously formidable, in that guard kept over this land of ours, in the black night; in the quiet recesses of the towns, and along the roads of the countryside, shadowy sentinels, strange sounds and murmurs in the streets, strange sounds and murmurs by the misty hedges, under the trees, in the winding lanes, between the fields, vapoury breaths, movements, tramplings, faint ebony gleams on steel helmets, little groups silhouetted against the sky, and every now and again searchlights that seem to throw pencils of light unto the very stars.

'How well they serve, who only watch and wait.' I have been wanting to say that ever since this war began. If there is anything which has made me proud of being a Britisher, proud of my people, that has filled me with confidence in our strength and resolution, that makes me certain of victory, it

is this Army of the Night. This army that waits, silent and ready, prepared for any emergency, keyed up to meet any shock. This army of the people, of citizens, watching over their homes; of workers, watching over their workplaces; of countrymen, watching over their land; ARP wardens going their rounds; fire-fighters and balloon barrage men; the first-aid men and nurses at their posts; anti-air :aft men by their guns; citizens and workers intermingled with the soldiers, all sprung from the people; on patrol through the city highways and byways, and all the roads that lead over the hills and down the valleys of Britain to the coast. And the coast, thronged with troops, lined with cannon courses, and, out at sea, the grey ships riding.

This fantastic night has countless eyes, countless arms ready to strike, a million stout hearts ready to repel the invader, all silent, save that the silence is sometimes disturbed by the drone of aircraft. Herr Hitler and Company, we are ready!

What tribute of praise can be made to those who give of their rest and sleep to maintain watch and ward over this island? To the fathers and husbands, keen to share with their sons and brothers in the Fighting Services, whatever dangers there be, whatever encounters may come? They are desperately resolved to protect their women and children, and they are invincibly determined to destroy those who would violate their homes and ravage their country. What tribute of praise do any of those require, who, through the lonely hours, stand to duty? Nevertheless, I feel that they deserve praise, encouragement, commendation, beyond words. To me there is something magnificent and supremely reassuring in this nocturnal spectacle of Britain prepared to meet and overcome the evil Nazi power and to fight to the death for freedom.

We are having air-raids; bombs are being dropped on ports, towns and villages. Men, women and children are being killed and maimed; peaceful homesteads are being shattered, sporadically, indiscriminately; we count the cost; we will remember. We are threatened with dark invasion. If that happens, the Army of the Night will strike. Britain will burst into flame. No hail that ever fell will equal the terrible hail that will then fall upon the Nazis. No lightnings that ever seared the sky will equal the lightnings that then will blast the invaders.

Meanwhile, how well they serve, who only watch and wait!

BBC Radio broadcast
24 July 1940

# Any Old Iron?

We started the old iron hunt by going down to the pit at the end of the field where peach tins, broken bottles and sardine cans have been dumped for some months, and I thought we should make, perhaps, three barrow-loads of it. Again I was wrong. For two evenings and most of Sunday one of us stood in the ever-deepening pit, grubbing for treasure and throwing it up. Five of us filled buckets and barrows, wheeled and carted the contents across a field and garden, and dumped them by the woodshed. We got up frying-pans, we got up kettles, we got up saucepans – tin hot-water bottles, iron piping, wire netting, ventilators, iron pipes, a clock, a cigarette case, two milk churns, biscuit tins, oil cans, watering cans, tin mugs, door hinges, meat covers, a paint-box, and two enormous churns, and we are not *yet* at the end of our digging. There is a whole second pit to be uncovered.

Meantime a curious thing happened. My country home is one of the houses in a tiny hamlet. There are also a farm, three cottages and another cottage four fields away. Now nobody had told anybody about the treasure hunt, but within half-a-day the entire hamlet was hard at work routing out old iron, with the children going to and fro like bees carrying honey. The treasures we were given! One cottage produced a huge iron bedstead and a sheet of corrugated iron; the farm gave us yet another milk churn and an old spring mattress; and the other cottages between them produced tins innumerable, broken cans, pails and piping, and glass bottles, which were a side-line in special charge of the children.

It is a funny thing, the treasure hunt instinct, and how you enjoy seeing if you can beat your neighbour to it. I got so keen that I began to loot the house itself, and I not only got out of it an enormous, rusty stove, three broken coal scuttles, screws, scrapers, mouse-traps, a radiator, a bell, broken spanners and the wrong half of a nut-cracker; but I finally got a man to knock down for me the entire brick baking-oven that was a mere antique, wasting space in the pantry, and out of it, besides wonderful brick rubble for the holes in the road, we got a firegrate, gratings and floorings.

Then Neville and Brian and Peter arrived from over the hill. Neville is five, Peter is four, Brian an experienced three-and-a-half. They are brothers—thin, gentle, cottage children, very shy, with dark, intelligent blue eyes. They had dragged with them an old perambulator full of tins and their toy bicycle. Certainly it had no saddle, a cockled wheel and only half a handlebar, but it was none the less a treasure. They hated parting with it, but they weren't proposing to miss the fun.

I praised them, of course. I said: 'Now that really *is* a good bit of war-work. That'll help to make a shell, you know!' and then I thought to myself that it was brutal of me to tell these small children what the old iron was to be used for. But I needn't have troubled, for as they trotted away – don't worry, they had their chocolate, even though the war was on! – I heard young England explaining the situation to youngest England. 'That's for Hitler, that is. If we 'it 'im first, 'e can't 'it us.'

Clemence Dane
*London Mercury*, 15 July 1940

*A group of young scrap-metal collectors in Chislehurst, Kent.*

—3—

# THE MEN THEY CALLED
# 'DOWDING'S CHICKS'

One of the most startling facts about the pilots who soared into the skies of Britain to take on the best the Luftwaffe had to offer in the summer of 1940 was that they were still very much an embryo force. As the former RAF pilot turned historian, Gavin Lyall, has most perceptively put it: 'At the time, Fighter Command still consisted mainly of gentlemen (the mobilised Auxiliary and volunteer weekend pilots) and players (pre-war career officers and NCOs). Although quite a number of already trained Polish and Czech pilots had just come on the strength, there had been no time for any wartime volunteers to be trained up from scratch. So the Command still retained much of its peacetime "cavalry" spirit: unquestionably brave, good at close parade formations, but lacking in modern tactics and generally poor at gunnery.'

As a 'weekend pilot' myself, it is not hard to imagine being in the place of those men, and the exhilaration they must have felt at the controls of the newly developed Spitfires and Hurricanes. But what we cannot so easily understand is that there was always the thought that death lay waiting for them, perhaps only minutes away in the sun-filled skies, each time they took off – from airfields really very little different to many of those still operated today by civilian flying clubs throughout the nation. This is a sobering fact, not to be underestimated or so lightly passed off as it often was by those young men half a century ago. 'Dowding's Chicks' Churchill later called them, referring specifically to the intakes of new recruits, many in their teens and early twenties, fledglings initially led by veterans – but all too soon, because of the heavy toll of the war, young men leading other young men.

The Fighter Command of the RAF was, in fact, less than four years old when the battle which would ensure its fame for ever began. Indeed, it had been set up on 14 July 1936 some three years after Hitler had come to power, and was widely regarded as very much the junior service among politicians and military men alike. All that was to change dramatically during the 'Spitfire Summer'.

From the very inception of Fighter Command, the Commander in Chief had been a Scotsman, Hugh Caswall Dowding – a rather austere, pipe-smoking figure nicknamed 'Stuffy' by his men, but later in 1943 to be knighted by his grateful country. Born in Moffat, Dumfries, Dowding had served with the Royal Flying Corps during the First World War and brought to his command a mixture of experience and sound common sense. He was a man with a highly individual turn of mind – as well as being a deeply although unconventionally religious person – and he had played a vital role in helping to shape the research and technical development of the RAF for some six years before assuming responsibility for the nation's air defences. He it was who had argued the service away from its reliance on wooden biplanes to the much faster all-metal monoplanes, and he had also been instrumental in taking on to the strength the Hurricanes and Spitfires which were to prove the glory of his fighting force.

It was Dowding, too, who had prevented the Government from sacrificing the RAF's remaining fighters in a vain attempt to save France earlier in 1940, sensing even then that a greater battle still lay ahead, not only for Britain but also for the free world, which would sooner or later be staged over his native land.

At the time when Dowding established his Fighter Command headquarters at Bentley Priory in Stanmore, Middlesex in 1936, the country's aerial defence consisted

*A group of Fighter Command pilots – 'Dowding's Chicks' – prepare for action.*

of just eleven squadrons of obsolescent biplanes. As can be imagined, it was no easy task to update this force into a serious challenge to the braggart Hitler, who was already claiming that his air power was superior to that of the RAF. But with a mixture of ingenuity, determination and faith, that is exactly what Dowding *was* able to do in the short time prior to those fateful days in July 1940.

It is an interesting but generally lesser known fact that the first 'fighter' missions flown against German forces following the declaration of war were actually made by members of the Auxiliary Air Force, men who had taken up flying because they loved it and who were as diverse in character as they were in their professions. Sent out to patrol the coasts on the look-out for enemy submarines, they became known as the 'Scarecrow Patrols' – a title given to them because their orders were to spot the U-Boats and then 'scare' them into submerging by simulating an attack!

From the moment hostilities were announced, it was not so much attack from the skies that the British Government most feared, rather that Hitler would initiate a ruthless submarine campaign around the British Isles – a threat that was realised by the almost immediate torpedoing of the passenger liner *Athenia*. The U-boats were evidently going to threaten British shipping at every turn and it was imperative that they should be spotted quickly whenever and wherever they appeared, to enable the Navy to swing into action its destroyers, armed with depths charges. Equally, because a submarine could not function at that time without raising its periscope above the surface to line up its victim, so if it could be forced to remain below, its effectiveness was much reduced.

And what better method of spotting the tell-tale periscopes than from an aircraft? But where were the machines to patrol the coasts of Britain – in particular those facing the North Sea and the Atlantic? All that were readily available for such duties in the autumn of 1939 were training aircraft, in particular the dual-control Tiger Moth, which had a top speed of about 110 miles an hour and was open to all the elements. At first sight this would seem an unpromising front-line aircraft, but it did have its own particular advantages.

And so, though the Tiger Moth was never intended for fighting or carrying bombs, the RAF turned to it in the opening months of the war to harry the U-Boats. The first Scarecrow Patrols were duly formed and sensibly based in Scotland. In the cockpits were the self-same builders, salesmen, accountants, schoolteachers, journalists and their like who had happily flown the little planes in times of peace and been quick to volunteer their services when called upon. Although the machines were camouflaged, no attempt was made to arm them, but each pilot was given a signal pistol and flares.

## RESERVED MEN...
## Do the war's biggest job

Flying in the R.A.F. is the most important war job a man can do — and so vital that you can even be released from reserved occupations to do it. So come forward now! Go to the R.A.F. Section, nearest Combined Recruiting Centre (address from any Employment Exchange), and say you want to volunteer for flying duties. If you cannot call, post this coupon (unsealed envelope, 1d. stamp). Age limits — 31 for Pilots, 33 for Observers.

*fly with the* **RAF**

To
Air Ministry Information Bureau, Kingsway, London, W.C.2. Please send "Flying Duties" leaflet.
I $\frac{am}{am\ not}$ in a reserved occupation.

AGE ...............

NAME........................................................

ADDRESS

PP/27/12

(above) *The call for men to join the RAF goes out –* and (right) *among those who answered it was the author's father (circled).*

Through the winter of 1939 the Scarecrow Patrols flew their tough and unglamorous missions, mostly in pairs and usually in sight of each other. They flew by day and night, and would 'buzz' any submarine they might come across – perhaps chanced upon lying on the surface, recharging its batteries – with the intention of making the captain believe that other planes were in the vicinity and forcing him into a hasty dive. The patrols also reported any 'sightings' to the nearest naval units. (With typical British ingenuity, some of the planes took carrier pigeons along with them for use in emergencies to get messages back to base.)

Not only were these missions hazardous – for a sub-marine might well stand its ground and open fire when it saw what kind of adversary it was facing – but with the coming of the freezing months of January and February 1940, when a large number of people actually died of cold in a Britain beset by impassable, snow-bound roads and homes paralysed by frozen pipes, the pilots in their open cockpits had to call on every ounce of endurance and resourcefulness to function in the sub-zero temperatures.

Because of the grey, churning waves of both the Atlantic and the North Sea, the Tiger Moths invariably had to fly low over the surface to spot the tell-tale 'white feather' made by the U-Boat periscopes. And that was not their only problem.

*An aircraft of the 'Scarecrow Patrol' catches a German submarine on the surface of the North Sea.*

*The Commander-in-Chief of Fighter Command, Hugh Dowding, in one of his Operations Rooms.*

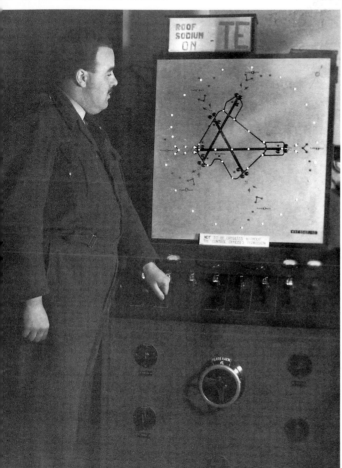

'It was exceptionally hard to turn one's head with all the protective clothing we had to wear,' Robert Williams, a former pilot of one of the squadrons, later recalled, 'let alone get at the signal pistol and flares. But all the difficulty was well worth while, because the uninterrupted view from those small planes could not be beaten, especially as there was no semi-opaque window to have to peer through, and the aircraft could be flown slowly.' (The Tiger Moth had an exceptionally slow flying speed of 55 miles an hour.)

The Scarecrow Patrols continued their missions until May 1940, and despite the appalling weather and the threat posed by the U-Boats, not a single man or machine was lost. Yet the pilots won none of the acclaim and honours that were to be heaped on their colleagues in the Battle of Britain – though they were clearly their forerunners in both spirit and courage. Some of these men did, however, go on to serve in the fully armed fighter squadrons that Dowding was moulding into his air defence force. And, as more than one patriot from north of the border has pointed out, it may not have been altogether a coincidence that some of the most successful Auxiliary squadrons of 'weekend pilots' during the Battle of Britain were those that came from Scotland. (See story 'Weekend Pilots' Successes'.)

While the Scarecrow Patrols were, in their own way, 'buying time' for Dowding around the northern coastline of Britain, he knew that another development was being put in place in the south that would immeasurably strengthen his hand when the Luftwaffe came. This was the world's first chain of radar stations, a highly secret defence system spread across southern England which could pinpoint enemy planes heading towards the country when they were still some distance away and then pass on the information to Fighter Command for action. It gave the RAF a unique advantage in early warning over anything the German forces possessed.

But every precious day that had passed since the fall of France without the Luftwaffe storming across the

*Behind the scenes at a Fighter Command station in the summer of 1940, from a collection of photographs belonging to the author's father. (top left) Flying Control at RAF Tempsford, near Bedford. (top right) Airfield Controller Sergeant Ron Richardson using an Aldis lamp to signal to pilots. (bottom left) Flight Lieutenant 'Tiny' Newton at the Tempsford Airfield Plan. (bottom right) A WAAF officer organising take-offs and landings in the Operations Room at Tempsford.*

BOULTON PAUL DEFIANT

SUPERMARINE SPITFIRE

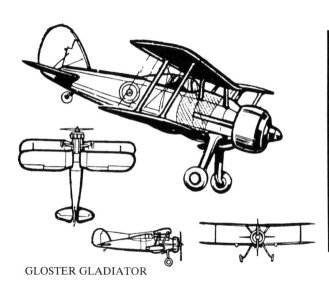

GLOSTER GLADIATOR

# THE OPPOSING AIRCRAFT

'The Opposing Aircraft' – these drawings of the Fighter Command and Luftwaffe aircraft which contested the Battle of Britain were first published in Flight magazine in July 1940 and later issued in one of the best-selling paperback books of the war, British, American, German and Italian Aircraft, which was revised and republished each year from 1940 to 1945.

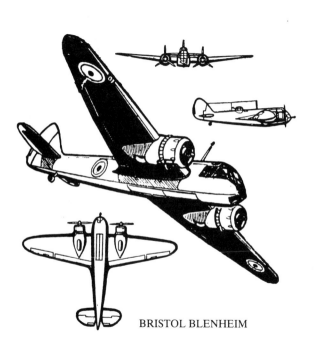

BRISTOL BLENHEIM

HAWKER HURRICANE

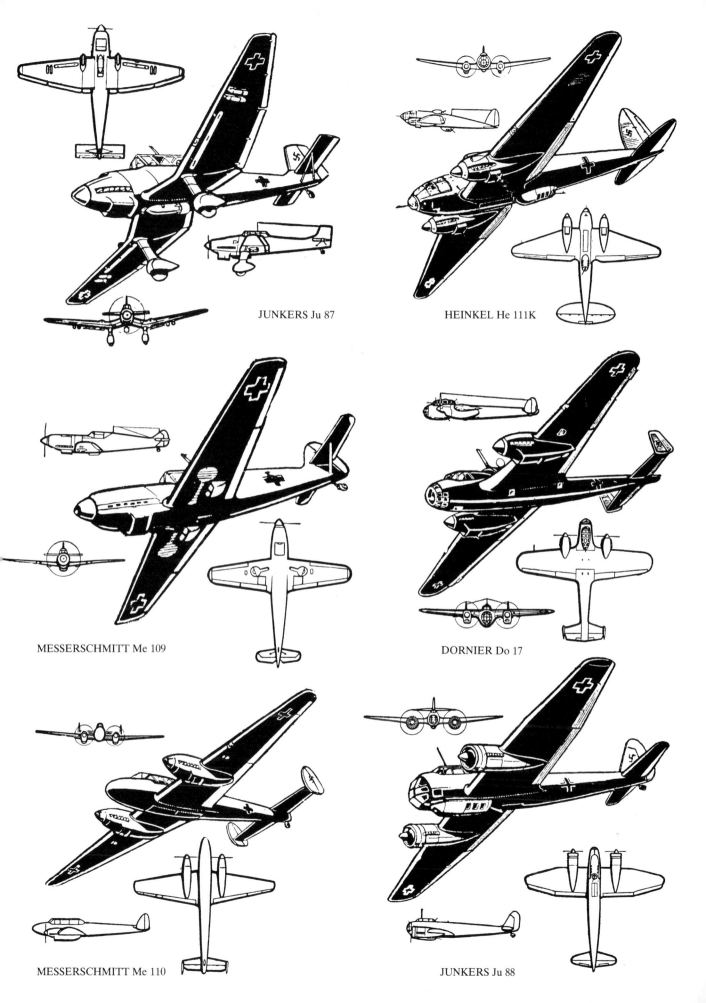

JUNKERS Ju 87

HEINKEL He 111K

MESSERSCHMITT Me 109

DORNIER Do 17

MESSERSCHMITT Me 110

JUNKERS Ju 88

Channel – held back, it later transpired, by Hitler's conviction that he could win a negotiated peace without bloodshed – enabled Dowding to increase the numbers of his planes and to train his men. Because of the losses of his squadrons in France – 450 fighters and 430 pilots in the preceding six weeks, virtually half his strength – the defence force for the homeland had initially consisted of only a few hundred Spitfires and Hurricanes, only half of which were then stationed in the most vulnerable south-east sector.

If the Luftwaffe *had* followed up its success in France with an immediate strike on England, Dowding had every reason to believe that what Churchill had predicted in his speech of 18 June would be 'their finest hour' might have ended very differently indeed. But the Germans did not come for almost a month after the Prime Minister's inspiring words were spoken – first delivered in Parliament and then broadcast by the BBC – and in that time the resolve of every man and woman in the nation had been immeasurably strengthened.

'What General Weygrand called the Battle of France is over,' Churchill said in those rich and redolent tones that no one who ever heard them has forgotten. 'I expect the Battle of Britain is about to begin. Upon this battle depends the survival of Christian civilisation. Upon it depends our own British life, and the long continuity of our institutions and our Empire.

'The whole fury and might of the enemy must very soon be turned upon us,' he continued. 'Hitler knows that he will have to break us in this island or lose the war. If we can stand up to him, all Europe may be free and the life of the world may move forward into broad, sunlit uplands. But if we fail, then the whole world, including the United States, including all that we have known and cared for, will sink into the abyss of a dark age made more sinister, and perhaps more protracted, by the lights of perverted science.'

The Prime Minister paused amidst the silence and rapt attention that greeted his words, and then coined his immortal phrase: 'Let us therefore brace ourselves to our duties, and so bear ourselves that, if the British Empire and its Commonwealth last for a thousand years, men will still say, "This was their finest hour".'

Hugh Dowding was as moved by his leader's words as anyone else in Britain, but perhaps realised better than most how heavily tilted the odds were and how much must depend on his 'Chicks'. But as the battle dawned in the weeks of July he could survey his forces with a mixture of increasing pride,even if tempered by understandable anxiety. Thanks to the super-human efforts of Beaverbrook and his workers, the C-in-C now had some 600 fighter planes at his command, the majority of which were Hurricanes. He had just over 1250 pilots fit for operation.

It is as well to pause here and reflect on the fact that Dowding's force consisted predominantly of Hurricanes, for it is a significant one in the way legend has remembered this summer of 1940. As the historian Richard Collier has written: 'British legend obstinately gives pride of place to the Vickers-Supermarine Spitfire, Mark I and II . . . but in fact only 19 Spitfire Squadrons took part in the Battle; at the peak, on August 30, exactly 372 Spitfires were ready for operations. By contrast, Hawker-Hurricane squadrons totalled 33 – with 709 planes available for front-line operations on August 30.'

Undeniable though these statistics are, and well though they may dispel a myth, they nevertheless overlook the far more significant fact that it was the faster, more impressive-looking and dashing Spitfire, newly arrived to the battleground in the skies, that in the people's eyes typified the British spirit of bravery and determination. It became an inspiration to all who saw it and, in turn, the symbol of the victory that was eventually won. Whatever facts may record – and as the title of this book implies – the climactic middle months of 1940 were undoubtedly the 'Spitfire Summer'.

At the beginning of that summer Dowding had divided Fighter Command into four groups: No. 13, covering the north-east of England and Scotland, under the command of Air Vice-Marshal R.E. Saul; No. 12, the north and Midlands led by Air Vice-Marshal Trafford Leigh-Mallory; No. 10, the West Country commanded by Air Vice-Marshal Quintin Brand; and No. 11, covering southern England and London, commanded by another man of Scottish ancestry, Air Vice-Marshal Keith Park.

No. 11 Group was the front-line force, consisting of nineteen squadrons totalling 200 aircraft. Six of these squadrons flew Spitfires, while the remaining thirteen all had Hurricanes. In Keith Park they had an outstanding and forthright leader who collaborated closely with Hugh Dowding to create a formidable tactical partnership united against the German aerial forces, now massed just 21 miles away across the Channel. In addition to Group 11, Fighter Command's other resources consisted of sixteen fighter squadrons of Hurricanes and Spitfires, six Blenheim squadrons, two squadrons of Defiants and a single squadron of six antiquated Gladiator biplanes based at Plymouth.

The opposing Luftwaffe was commanded by Field Marshal Hermann Goering, whose forces were divided into three groups: Luftflotte 2, ranged across northern Germany, Holland, Belgium and the north of France, commanded by Field Marshal Hans Kesselring and based in Brussels; Luftflotte 3, covering the remainder of France and southern Germany, led by Field Marshal Hugo Sperrle in Paris; and Luftflotte 5, based in

*Reichsmarschall Hermann Goering makes his plans for the Luftwaffe's attacks on Britain with Field Marshal Hugo Sperrle* (holding map).

Scandinavia under the command of General Peter Stumpff in Oslo. The combined strength of Kesselring's and Sperrle's forces amounted to 800 single-engined fighters (Messerschmitt BF109s and Junkers JU87s), 250 twin-engined fighters (Messerschmitt BF110s), 1130 medium bombers (Dornier DO17s and Heinkel HE111s), 320 dive bombers (Junkers JU88s) and about 60 reconnaissance aircraft of various types. Stumpff, in the north, had on call 130 medium bombers, 50 reconnaissance aircraft and 40 twin-engined fighters.

As can be seen from this line-up, not only was the Luftwaffe numerically stronger than Fighter Command, but it was also flying planes that had been tried and tested in actual combat situations – earlier in

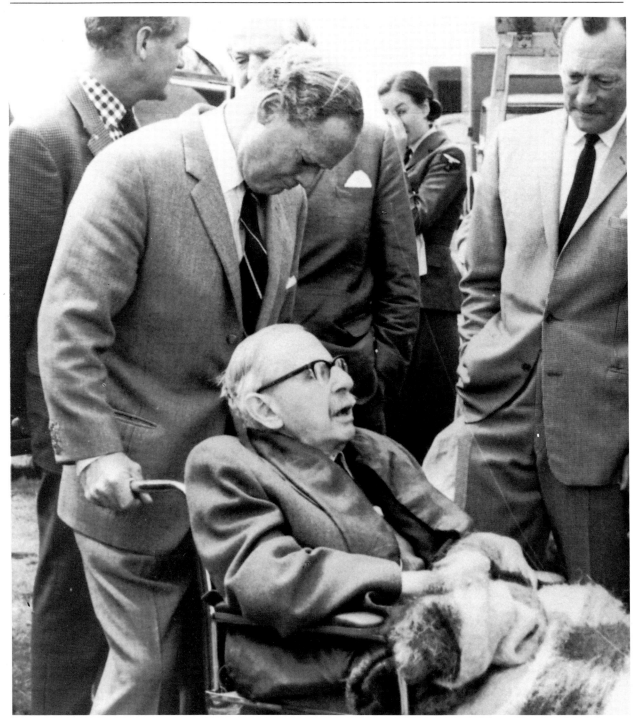

the Spanish Civil War and most recently in the attacks on Poland. The vast majority of its pilots were, as a consequence, far more experienced than their British counterparts. But veterans though they might be, for the first time they were to be asked to fight over a resolutely protected island against a defence system that would see them coming no matter what evasive action they might take.

However, such facts were unknown to the strutting, grandiloquent figure of Goering as he looked from France across the Channel at perhaps the richest prize

that he had so far been asked to seize. While to many the Field Marshal appeared a fat, vain and rather ridiculous figure whose self-esteem blunted his capacity as a strategist because he believed nothing to be beyond his air force, he was none the less trusted by Hitler and hero-worshipped by his men. In fact, Goering had been one of the first infantry officers to fight on the Western Front in the First World War, and in 1915 had been transferred to the German Air Force where he became an ace pilot and commander of the famous 'Death Squadron'. The pilots of the Luftwaffe who

*The late Lord Dowding on the set of the film* Battle of Britain *in 1969 with two of his leading fighter aces of the summer of 1940, Wing Commander Douglas Bader (*left*) and Wing Commander Stanford Tuck.*

went to war under his leadership in 1939 knew his record well, and offered immediate and unquestioning obedience.

A string of early successes in Europe added to Goering's prestige, and in June 1940 Hitler made him Marschal of the Reich, the first (and as it transpired, only) holder of the rank. And so it was at the pinnacle of his military career that Goering faced Britain across the narrow stretch of water. The battle that followed was to prove the turning point in his career.

Goering had, though, no premonitions of this in July 1940; and before the month was out, with the battle hardly fully joined, he was already looking forward to victory, as he told foreign journalists. An American reporter, Carl von Weigand, who spoke to him during a conducted tour of France, filed to the *New York Times* the following comments made to him by the Luftwaffe chief on Tuesday 31 July.

'The battle is still very young. Its future cannot yet be foreseen, but it has certain limits. The German Air Force dominates the North Sea and the Channel, but on the wide oceans our Navy still has its tasks to fulfil. On the Continent, Germany dominates the air. We shall keep this domination. You may not believe it, but my Air Force is stronger today than it was at the beginning of the offensive in the West. Since September 1939, more than 2000 aeroplanes have fallen into German hands.'

At Bentley Priory, Commander-in-Chief Dowding with his much smaller force must have been surprised when he read this exaggerated claim. But action rather than words was his motto at this time, and the researcher will look in vain for quotes in the press in July 1940 from the leader of Britain's few. Indeed, it was not until the end of the war that Dowding went on record about his emotions and convictions at this crucial moment. I had the privilege of meeting this fine old man in 1969, just a year before his death, during the making of the film *The Battle of Britain*. His comments, made then with the hindsight of almost thirty years, were fascinating.

'I remember I was tremendously overpowered by the importance of the task I had been given,' he said, speaking slowly from the wheelchair to which he was confined. 'As far as responsibility was concerned, my feeling was one of hope that I would be worthy of the opportunity I had been given of upholding the spirit of my pilots, and that I should not be letting down Fighter Command or the Air Force – or, indeed, the country.'

Lord Dowding – as he was by then – recalled that it was Churchill who had coined the name 'Battle of Britain', which he felt was a very apt nomenclature. But he had sensed much earlier that a battle was coming.

'I felt a great responsibility on my shoulders, part of which was to prepare the country for the eventual outcome of this battle. I remember I did put up a little prayer to heaven that I might be worthy of it. I know I couldn't have carried on without some basic belief of that kind, though my own belief is not pegged into any particular hole. It's absurd to say: this is right and this is wrong. If we call the controlling force God, then I pray to God now, and I did in those days thirty years ago.'

When Dowding spoke of the men of Fighter Command, his face broke into a mellow smile at the memory. 'They were a wonderful set of fellows, my pilots. I don't think there has ever been anything quite like the same light-heartedness and spirit in the face of an issue that was anything but light-hearted. You only have to think of the way they made jokes about things and created their own slang language to gather what I mean! [See the panel on RAF slang]. But we were all of us alive to the fact that it was a deadly game. And I felt instinctively as I had these fellows gathered around me, that whatever happened they wouldn't let me down.

'I don't think my pilots were a unique generation,' he went on. 'They were the last of a breed. Their loyalty was due to a tradition that was handed down – and to the conditions they were fighting under. I've thought about this a lot since – but at the time we were too busy to analyse such things! If those lads hadn't had this absolute refusal to be daunted, they would never have put up with the casualty rate they had to suffer.'

Lord Dowding also talked about his special relationship with Air Vice-Marshal Keith Park, and revealed that his tactics in battle had not always been accepted by others. 'I could always speak openly to Keith Park because he had my complete confidence. But there were others who were hostile to me, and I had to speak to them in a quite different way. In fact, I used to brief my group commanders separately. But I never lost sight of the fact that my prime duty was to my pilots.'

Reflecting for what may perhaps have been almost the last time on his part in the battle that changed history, Lord Dowding added, without a trace of false modesty: 'I know that being a leader means you have something the others haven't got. I feel that some men are born to lead. It is in their blood. Yet looking back I believe I was lucky in a way: there has probably never been a leader in any important war who had the opportunity to step on to such a prepared stage when the critical moment came.'

And so, firm in his determination and heartened by the resolve of his pilots as well as the nation as a whole, Dowding stepped on to this 'prepared stage' and braced himself for the onslaught – the signs of which were growing ever stronger with the passing days of that long, hot July.

*" Quick—follow that Heinkel!"*

A humorous comment on the 'Weekend Pilots' by
another of the war's famous cartoonists, 'Fougasse'
(Kenneth Bird), from Punch, 1 May 1940.

## WEEKEND PILOTS' SUCCESSES

Pilots of the Auxiliary Squadrons of the RAF
Fighter Command have now shot down well over
200 enemy aircraft. These are the men who trained
in their spare time, mostly at weekends, and
became known as the 'Weekend Pilots'.

These men were drawn from almost all walks of
life, and have fought alongside the regular
squadrons in every phase of the air war, in home
defence, in offensive patrols over the Low
Countries, above the Dunkirk sands, and more
recently in the large-scale battles over the English
Channel.

Two Scottish Spitfire Squadrons which have
been engaged since the start of the war in
defending their country are the only Auxiliary
Fighter Squadrons which have never fought over
France or the Low Countries. In spite of the fact
they have not had the opportunities for engaging
large formations of the enemy, one of them has a
higher total of raiders brought down than any
other auxiliary squadron.

A Squadron Leader of one of the Auxiliary
Squadrons described a recent engagement with a
large force of German aircraft over the English
Channel in these words.

'It was a terrific scrum,' he said. 'There were six
of us split up into two formations of three. The
situation looked pretty grim. The best we could
hope for was to upset them a bit. We did!

'I ordered my formation into a line astern. The
enemy bombers were just about to dive onto a
convoy. As the Dorniers attacked, I singled out one
and gave him a short burst. I had to pull away
immediately because I was in close line abreast
with the following Dornier.

'I came in again to attack another Dornier, and
had just opened fire when tracers started whistling
past me. I took immediate and evasive action. My
starboard aileron got a terrific crack. It partially
jammed, making my Spitfire difficult for me to
control. There was nothing for me to do but to beat
it home. I spoke to the other members of the
Squadron and told them not to hang about.

'I don't know what happened to the other
Dorniers I attacked; there were too many Huns
about to wait and see. They were diving one after
another onto the convoy. The ships were blazing
away at them. It was quite a show, all right!'

*Daily Mail*
**15 August 1940**

# RAF SLANG

Many of the squadrons in the Air Force have their own slang words and a stranger in the mess could hear conversation going on without understanding a word of it. How could he know, when he heard a young pilot-officer say that he was 'browned-off', that he meant that he was depressed or fed-up? And he might well fail to understand somebody saying: 'I saw a wizard job in the village this morning.' How could he suspect that the pilot-officer meant that he had seen a beautiful girl? There are even class distinctions in the use of slang in the Service, and the fitters and riggers and other members of the ground staff frequently refer to aircraft as 'kites'. They will say: 'You sort of become attached to the kite on which you are working just like a groom with his horse.' The pilot himself scorns the word 'kite'. He prefers 'aircraft'.

I went to a station on the East Coast a few weeks ago and talked to a rigger who was the wag of the Squadron. Let me repeat a piece of his conversation. He said, 'I was a bit browned-off when we were stationed at *X*. But when we moved to *Y*, there was bags of excitement. The first day, our kites took off to intercept some Germans'. He went on: 'When the raid was over we felt a bit browned-off because we were hungry, so we found a chicken and I borrowed the grid – you know, the boot-scraper – from the doorstep and four of us cooked it over a fire. It took three-and-a-half hours to cook, but it was wizard when it was finished.' Most expressive! You can almost smell that chicken!

Most of the everyday slang words of the Air Force are very descriptive. When a man is making a fuss, they say he is 'getting into a flap', or that he is 'flapping'. The ornate gold oak leaves on the peak of an Air Commodore's hat are called 'scrambled eggs' – quite good. A glaring error is a 'black'. 'I have put up a black,' they will say. But one of the best phrases is used to describe some problem which they have mastered. They say, 'I have got that buttoned up.' There is one phrase, most descriptive, but with an origin I have never been able to trace. When a senior officer reprimands his junior, the culprit says, 'He tore a strip off me.' There you have the full value of slang. However obscure the origin of the phrase, I can imagine nothing which could better describe one's state of mind after being harangued by one's betters – a strip torn off.

The Royal Air Force also falls in love with words and makes them fashionable for a time. Like a flash, the phrase 'wicked enemy' had swept through the Service. 'I met the wicked enemy.' 'I wonder if the wicked enemy will arrive tonight.' 'The wicked enemy appeared out of the clouds.' It seems to be a very mild adjective, but you will hear it used, at the moment, in almost every station in the country. In a month's time, it may be forgotten, and another adjective will take its place.

A Service which lives so vitally as the Royal Air Force naturally creates a language of its own. But what is interesting is to watch the way in which the public slowly accepts and uses the words, so that they slowly become part of the language and, at last, achieve the honour of being included in dictionaries or even of being used as headings in *The Times*!

Hector Bolitho
*The Spectator*, July 1940

# A GLOSSARY OF RAF SLANG

**Adj** Adjutant

**Balloonatics** Personnel in balloon command

**Beat up** To attack, either playfully or seriously, any place or thing

**Big noise** Important person (frequently ironic)

**Bird-dog, to** To steal another chap's girl

**Bit of fluff** A girl (usually the fluffy kind)

**Black, a** Something badly done, a 'bad show'

**Blackouts or twilights** WAAF-issue panties (black in colour)

**Blitz, a solid lump of** Large formation of enemy aircraft

**Bog rat** Recruit (a bog rat being the lowest animal the RAF can imagine)

**Blood wagon or meat wagon** Ambulance

**Bought it** Was killed

**Brassed off** Variant of 'browned off'

**Brolly** Parachute

**Browned off** Fed up

**Bus driver** Bomber pilot

**Buttoned up** Job properly completed, 'mastered'

**CO** Commanding Officer

**Civvie Street** Civilian life

**Civvies** Civilian clothes

**Clobber** To beat unmercifully, to destroy. (A plane badly shot up was frightfully 'clobbered'.)

**Completely cheesed** Completely at a loss

**Completely surrounded** No hope at all

**Crabbing along** Flying near the ground or water

**Crate** An aeroplane

**Cyphereen** Senior Cypher Officer (WAAF)

One of several booklets published later in the war to
cater to the public interest in RAF slang. This
paperback, illustrated by David Langdon, was issued in
1943.

**Dead-beat** RAF non-flying personnel
**Deck, crack down on** To crash-land an aeroplane
**Deck, down to the** Flying close to the water
**Dim** Slow-witted
**Ding bat, to go like a** To travel at almost incredible speed
**Do a bunk** To leave without permission
**Drill, the right** Correct method of doing anything
**Drink, go down in the** To come down in the sea
**Dud** Applied to weather when unfit to fly
**Duff gen** Incorrect information
**Dust bin** Rear gunner's lower position on an aircraft
**Dwaaf** Director of WAAFs

**Erk, an** Aircraftsman or Aircraftswoman – the rank in the RAF–WAAF corresponding to a private in the army

**Fan** The propeller
**Fireworks, Mr** Armaments Officer
**Flak** Anti-aircraft fire
**Flannel, to** To toady, to seek favour by fawning
**Flap** A disturbance, general excitement
**Flat out** Completely exhausted

**Gen (pronounced 'jen')** Information of any kind
**George** The automatic pilot
**Get cracking** Get going
**Get weaving** Get cracking
**Glamour badge** Brevet
**Glamour boys** Fighter pilots
**Gong** Medal
**Gravy** Petrol, gasoline
**Greenhouse** Cockpit cover
**Gremlins** The 'little men' of the RAF
**Groupy** Group Captain

**Harbour Master** Commanding Officer of a Station
**Have had it** To have been killed, or, said ironically, meaning just the opposite, meaning *not* to have had something
**Hedge-hopping** Flying so low the aircraft appears to be flying over hedges
**Hooching** Pub-crawling, drinking at public houses, bars

**Jink** Sharp manoeuvre, sudden evasive action by aircraft

**Kee-*toi*-ing** Crash of any kind – usually a sudden crash in love
**Kipper Kite** Coastal Command aircraft which convoy fishing fleets in the North and Irish Seas
**Kite** Aeroplane

**Lay on, to** To arrange anything, to produce anything
**Left, right and centre** All over the place

**Mae West** Life-saving stole or waistcoat, inflated if wearer falls into the sea
**Mickey Mouse** Bomb-dropping mechanism

**Office** Cockpit of aircraft
**On your knees** Too tired to stand
**One Pipper** Second Lieutenant (Army)
**Operational** Anything that actually does its job: an aeroplane, a fountain pen, shoes, the weather, anything at all can be operational – or not

**Pack up** To cease to function
**Pancake** To land an aeroplane; formerly a crash landing, now any landing at all
**Peel off, to** To break formation
**Pickled as a newt** Tiddly, intoxicated
**Piece of cake** Gift from the gods. (A Hun aircraft easily shot down, a girl easy to meet – each was a 'piece of cake'.)
**Play pussy, to** Hide in the clouds
**Pleep** A squeak, rather like a high note klaxon
**Plonk** Recruit
**Pulchritude** Wizard wench, a glamour girl
**Pull your finger out!** Stop loafing!
**Put your props up** To be promoted to Leading Aircraftsman or Leading Aircraftswoman, at which time a propeller insignia is sewn on the sleeve
**Prang** Crash – usually meaning to crash an aircraft, though one can be pranged, broken up by a girl
**Pug away** Continue to fire, keep after target
**Pukka gen** Accurate information
**Pulpit** Cockpit of aircraft

**Queen Bee** Senior WAAF (Administrative) Officer on a Station
**Quick squirt** Short, sharp burst of fire
**Quickie** A quick anything – burst of fire, drink, love affair, etc.

**Rang the bell** Got good results
**Ring conscious** Conscious of rank. (Rank in the RAF and WAAF is designated by width and number of rings on the cuff of the tunic.)
**Rings** Rank designation on officer's cuff
**Ropey** Uncomplimentary adjective – ropey landing, ropey type, ropey evening, etc.

**Screaming downhill** Executing power dive
**Scrub, to** To wash out
**Second Dickey** Second pilot
**Shaken** To be suddenly and severely taken aback
**Shaky do** Dangerous operation
**Shogging** Making love
**Shooting a line** Exaggerated talk, generally about one's own powers
**Shot down in flames** Crossed in love; severely reprimanded
**Show – 'good', 'bad', 'poor'** Anything can be a 'show' – dinner party, dogfight, trip to London, etc.
**Sicky-dog** To feel ill
**Snake about** Operational aerobatics
**Spun in** Any bad mistake
**Sprog** Brand new uniform; newly commissioned officer
**Squaaf** Squadron Officers (WAAF)
**Stationmaster** Commanding Officer of Station
**Stooge** A stand-in, a deputy, one who does something for someone else
**Stooging about** Patrolling, flying slowly over an area, usually looking for trouble

**Tail-end Charlie** Rear gunner in a large bombing aircraft, or the pilot of rear aircraft in formation
**Tapes** Non-commissioned officers' stripes
**Tear a strip off** Reprove severely
**Tick off** Reprove (less than 'tear a strip off')
**Tiddly** Intoxicated
**Touch bottom** Crash
**Toys** A great deal of training equipment is termed 'toys'
**Train, driving the** Leading more than one squadron into battle
**Type** Classification – usually referring to people: good, bad, ropey, etc.

**U.S.** Unserviceable – anything at all can be 'U.S.': weather, aeroplane, etc.

**View** RAF personnel always take a 'view' of things – good, poor, dim, etc.

**Weave, to** To take evasive action in aircraft – not quite so sudden or violent as jink
**Weaving uneven course for home** Tiddly, half seas over
**Wizard** Really first class, superlative, attractive, ingenious – anything deserving, or getting, highest praise
**Wizzed as a bee** Tiddly
**Worthy type** Said ironically and sarcastically of solemn and self-righteous individual

# —4—

# MRS CARDWELL CAPTURES A GERMAN AIRMAN

Nora Cardwell was a typical no-nonsense York-shirewoman who was tackling the problems of being at war in July 1940 with the same resolution that she and her husband, Norman, had run their farm near Scarborough for the past twenty years. Life had always been demanding on Nora, and the long hours and often back-breaking work the farm entailed – not to mention raising her family of three children – made her doubly sure that she was not going to let this man Hitler interrupt *her* routine. Especially as Norman now often had to be away from the farm to carry out his duties as an officer in the local Home Guard.

Though Nora, who was just turned forty-five, had been in her late teens when the First World War broke out, her memories of that terrible conflict had not alto-gether faded, for she had lost several relatives, including a brother. But she had always been a woman who made sure her head ruled her heart, and when in the previous September she had listened on the radio to Neville Chamberlain announcing that the country was once again at war with Germany, she allowed herself only a brief moment of sadness before steeling herself to be ready for whatever fate might have in store for her and her family.

Nora and her husband had agreed that although Norman was now in his late forties and obviously too old for the Services, he could still put his knowledge of

machinery and sound common sense to good use in the local Defence Volunteers. For her part, Nora had joined the WVS which, although it demanded some of her time, did allow her to continue the day-to-day running of the farm and the organisation of the handful of workers the couple employed.

In fact the war barely intruded on the Cardwells that first winter, what with the terrible snow which brought life to a standstill on land and for a time actually froze the North Sea off the coast of Scarborough, although Nora listened to the radio and read the newspapers and was aware of the German forces getting ever closer to England. It was not until spring had fairly bloomed and she was busy on the land that she had a taste of what might be in store for the nation, when the first German reconnaissance planes were spotted high over the north-east coast.

In May and June, Nora several times saw what she knew must be British planes racing to intercept German intruders, though she could see little more than vapour trails and only very faintly hear the sound of gunfire that followed. However, all that changed dramatically on Sunday 7 July.

The morning was another clear and bright one, the sun shining down on the fields of ripening corn as Nora went about her usual chores around the farm. Norman had left the house earlier – there was talk of more German planes coming over and he thought he should be at the local headquarters. At about 10.30 a.m., not long after she had gone into the kitchen to make a cup of tea, Nora suddenly heard a banging at the back door. Opening the door, she found one of her workmen almost out of breath and gesticulating wildly up at the sky.

*A photographer was on hand to record this moment in July 1940 when a German pilot shot down over England was given first aid by his captors.*

Nora herself tells the story of the day she captured a Nazi. 'One of the farm men was standing at the door,' she said. 'He blurted out that some German parachutists were coming down. I asked him if he had seen any sign of a battle in the sky, but he shook his head. My first thought was that the parachutists might be from a plane that had been shot down. But I had also heard stories that the Germans were planning to invade us. Could it be happening *now*, I wondered?'

Not a woman to panic, Nora decided to ring Norman at the local headquarters. Hurrying from the kitchen into the hallway, she lifted the receiver of the telephone. It sounded strangely quiet against her ear. She tapped the receiver cradle several times, but nothing happened.

'It was obviously out of order,' she recalled. 'But *what* a time to have happened! I didn't think about it then, but I suppose if there had been an invasion the first thing the Germans would have done would be to cut the telephone wires. Anyway, I decided to send one of the farm boys on his bicycle to fetch the police, who were closer to the farm than Norman's headquarters.'

As soon as the boy had been found, given his instructions and had pedalled off, Nora decided that she herself must take some action. She remembered being told that parachutists had to be dealt with very quickly before they had a chance to do any damage.

'Well, I went out into the garden determined to do *something*,' she said, 'and what should be the first thing I saw but this airman, in German uniform, limping across the paddock towards the house! For a moment I stood there. I knew there were people about, but how could I attract their attention? I even thought about going back for one of my husband's guns – but suppose the German was a better shot? So I just walked across to the man and told him to put his hands up!'

Nora remembered that her heart was pumping wildly in her chest as she looked at the German airman. His face was ashen and there was blood on his clothes. It seemed very obvious to her that he must have come from a crashed aircraft. (He had, in fact, jumped from a Junkers 88.) Then her heart missed a beat altogether when she noticed he had an automatic pistol in a holster at his side.

'He stared at me and again I told him to put up his hands. He did not understand me, so I made the sign with my hands. Very slowly, he raised his hands in the air. I pointed to the gun in his belt and said, "I want that." I can't tell you how relieved I was when he handed it over!'

Nora remembers that the German was about 6 feet 3 inches tall and looked about twenty-five years old. There seemed very little fight left in him. 'I walked with the airman in front of me to the road where I hoped that help would come when the boy reached the police station and told them,' she added. 'We waited there for about half an hour before the police and soldiers arrived and took him

away.'

It was only later that Sunday, when Nora was sharing a welcome cup of tea with Norman who had hurried home after hearing about the 'arrest', that the brave housewife began to appreciate just what a risk she had taken. But no such thought had entered her mind – and in that she was just like tens of thousands of other men and women in Britain in the weeks that followed when the Nazi raiders developed from being just an idea mentioned on the radio or in the newspapers (or occasionally even glimpsed high in the sky) to become actual machines of death arriving right on their very doorsteps.

A week later, for instance, in the south-east, a woman captured not one but five German airmen, according to the following report from *The Times* of Monday 15 July, which, in the tradition of the time, had been censored, deleting names and actual locations.

'In a south-eastern area which has been visited by

*A fourteen-year-old girl and a milkman took prisoner the two-man crew of this twin-engined ME 110 when it crash-landed on the south-east coast in July 1940.*

enemy aircraft several times, it was learned today of incidents which show the cool way in which people living in the area regard the German incursions.

'One enemy bomber, after being badly damaged by British fighters, came down, and a woman living in a nearby cottage was instrumental in the capture of the crew of five. After the machine landed, it caught fire. Seeing one of the crew get out of the fuselage and start trying to release the others, the woman ran up to him and said, "Here, you, stay put. Stop just as you are until I come back." She hurried off to obtain help, and the imprisoned men were all rescued from the blazing machine, all five being taken prisoner.'

A footnote to this same story reported that on the previous Friday night, a village innkeeper and a house painter had also captured the crew of a German aeroplane which had crashed in a field in Kent after having been riddled with bullets by a British fighter. And as if to show that it was not only people living in the countryside who could show such pluck, the *News Chronicle* of 26 July headlined a report from Bristol: 'Housemaid Captures German Airman'.

'One of three German airmen who landed by parachute in a south-west district last night was captured by a housemaid who remembered while she was sheltering in a dug-out that she had left a gas iron on. Ignoring machine gun fire and explosions, she was leaving the shelter to turn off the gas when the airman landed almost beside her! Seeing that he was badly affected by the crash, she took him into the house and gave him a whisky.

'Four men had actually leapt from the German bomber, which came down with its starboard engine shot away,' the report added, 'but the parachute of one failed to open. The other two were arrested by the Home Guard, which was quickly on the scene.'

A fascinating selection of photographs of captured German airmen, 'most of them remarkable for their youth and humble rank', published by the Illustrated London News *in September 1940.*

The maid's humane act in giving the German airman whisky undoubtedly came as something of a surprise to him – for according to reports in the press in July 1940, Nazi airmen feared more for their lives from being captured than in battle! A typical report from the *Daily Mirror* of Thursday 15 August, headlined 'German Airman's Plea', will illustrate the point.

'A German airman of about 18 who baled out from his machine in the south-east of England produced a photograph from his breast pocket when he was caught. He held it up and said, "This is my mother." He explained that he had been told that if he showed a photograph of his mother the English would not shoot him.'

*The Times* was evidently intrigued by such stories and on Saturday 27 July carried an interesting article about what it called 'alleged British atrocities'. The paper had unmasked the German propaganda machine at work yet again.

'In an effort to stir up feelings of even deeper hatred

Crowds gathered from miles around when this Heinkel 111 bomber crashed on a hillside near the village of Humble in East Lothian. Of the crew of four, two were killed and one wounded.

against this country,' *The Times* stated, 'the Nazi authorities have concocted a series of alleged British atrocities in the war. German airmen, soldiers and seamen are warned that if they are taken prisoner by the British they will not only be half starved but they will be subjected to all sorts of gross indignities and will even be ill-treated in a manner reminiscent of the Spanish Inquisition!

'The extent to which even the most blatant falsehoods are believed by the Germans is shown by the relief displayed by prisoners when they find they are very well treated in this country. Some airmen captured recently after having been shot down over and around the British Isles have expressed surprise that they have not been brutally treated. When they have been assured that no harm will befall them, their surprise has turned to anger against the authorities who have deliberately lied to them. Two airmen brought in yesterday expected unpleasant and speedy deaths. One said he had been told his throat would be cut; the

other said he had been warned he would be bumped off on sight.

'The pilot of a crashed Messerschmitt captured a few days ago was also convinced that he was to be shot,' the paper concluded. 'Some of the alleged British "atrocities" would be amusing but for the tragic fact that they are widely believed in Germany.'

Other facts that were also beginning to be deliberately distorted were the figures for aeroplanes destroyed – and the British authorities were as much to blame in this respect as those in Germany. Both sides were naturally anxious to minimise their losses, though in Fighter Command's case, with their much more slender resources to begin with, this may be easier to understand.

Consensus of opinion has it that the first shots in the 'Battle of Britain' proper occurred at around two o'clock on the afternoon of Wednesday 10 July – coincidentally just as Lord Beaverbrook was launching his appeal for aluminium for Spitfires. Six Hurricanes

# To the Country People of Britain

YOU have a great duty — the duty of keeping the roads free for our troops, no matter what happens.

Should parachutists land, or should enemy forces push inland from our coasts, some less-brave people may be tempted to flee from threatened villages and towns.

Don't do it. Stay where you are. This is not just advice, it is an order from the Government. The greatest harm any man or woman could do to Britain at such a time would be to clutter up the roads, and so hinder our own troops advancing to drive the enemy out.

In France refugees crowding the roads made it impossible for the army to bring up reinforcements. So France was lost!

*This must not happen here.* Remember, you will be far safer from bombing and machine-gunning downstairs in your own home than you would be on the open roads.

Remember, too, the Home Guard will be defending your village, and the Army will be defending your country. They need the roads.

# ... that's why you must STAY PUT

of No. 32 Squadron patrolling 10,000 feet over a convoy in the English Channel were suddenly confronted by close on a hundred German fighters and bombers about to launch themselves at the ships. Three of the patrol, all men on loan from the Fleet Air Arm – Flying Officer J.B.W. Humpherson, Sub-Lieutenant G.R. Bulmer and Sergeant L. Pearce – peeled away and opened fire on the massed ranks of Germans, one of which, a Dornier 17, fell into the sea, thereby enabling the British to claim the credit (if such it can be described) of 'starting' the Battle of Britain. (The official record of this day describes the action as a 'brisk skirmish' in which Sir Keith Park's fighters engaged Air Marshal Kesselring's forces, causing the loss of three and possibly more German aircraft.)

That evening, Members of Parliament sitting in the Commons were informed of the air battle that had taken place over the Channel and told that German bombers were at that very moment making their way towards British towns. 'Tonight,' said Sir Edward Grigg, the Parliamentary Secretary to the Ministry of Information, 'thousands of our soldiers will be on alert waiting for an attack which may come in several places at dawn.'

It was actually to be three more days before Charles Gardner's description of a fight over the Channel made the public as a whole aware of the battle that was now under way, and three more weeks before the bombardment of the towns that Sir Edward feared. In the interim – from 11 to 24 July – Kesselring and Sperrle continued their attacks on the coastal convoys, losing a total of 93 aircraft to Fighter Command's 48. Nevertheless, they succeeded in first causing the British Admiralty to suspend all merchant traffic through the Straits in daylight from 26 July, and secondly, from 29 July, in closing the Channel to destroyers in daylight. Only minesweepers were thereafter allowed to battle on to keep a passageway open.

It was on 11 July, the day after the three Hurricanes' successful attack on the German Dornier over the Channel, that Fighter Command suffered its first losses in this phase of the war. Again it was Hurricanes involved, this time from 501 Squadron, and during an engagement with ten enemy bombers and twenty escorting fighters, a plane piloted by Sergeant J.L. Dixon was shot down in the sea and lost.

Only a few minutes after this fight, six Spitfires from 609 Squadron arrived on the scene, and during a frantic

dog-fight two of the aircraft flown by Flight Lieutenant Barran and Pilot Officer Mitchell were sent spinning in flames into the murky grey waters of the Channel.

However, despite the flurry of activity in the second week of July, there was a general lack of concentrated action throughout the rest of the month, the Germans evidently working on a policy of appearing just often enough and in sufficiently large numbers to demonstrate their strength. Primarily, too, they concentrated their activities over the Channel and around the British coastline, for already they had learnt to respect the accuracy of the anti-aircraft gunners on land.

But what the population of Britain did not see in terms of enemy aircraft streaming overhead was more than made up by the balloon barrage which was now up in the skies in strength to hamper dive-bombing and low-level attacks. A few of these 'blimps', as they were known, occasionally carried crews of observers, but they were mostly unmanned. Interestingly, the origin of the term 'when the balloon goes up', now in popular usage to refer to something dramatic happening, can be traced back to this period.

The RAF had 55 squadrons in its Balloon Command, consisting of about 1500 balloons which offered quite extensive coverage against aerial attack. They became a familiar sight across the country, hanging like giant chrysalises usually about 5000 feet above ground level. The general public regarded them in terms of amusement that sometimes bordered on the obscene when describing their movements, but there is no doubt they were a comfort to those living in parts of the country which had neither aircraft bases nor anti-aircraft units to provide protection.

To German pilots the balloons had a considerable nuisance value – the crew of one hanging over Dover actually shot down a Messerschmitt 109 – and not a few of them were distracted from their missions in order to try to explode the lumbering behemoths. One such display of temper was witnessed by Anthony Eden, Churchill's right-hand man and then Secretary of State for War, while on an inspection visit to Dover.

'It was on a Sunday evening,' he was to recall later, 'and I had just walked on to the promenade of the Dover sea front to inspect the AA guns. There was a huge barrage balloon hovering over the harbour. All of a sudden, the AA guns began firing and I could see they were shooting at an ME109 which was coming in towards us over the Channel.

'At this, the German pilot swung around and then turned in on the balloon and released round after round of fire at it. It was rather like an angry bee trying to sting an elephant! Obviously the balloon could not withstand the attack, and riddled with incendiary bullets it fell in flames into the sea. The raider then flew

*An appeal to patriotism which the Ministry of Information published in newspapers and magazines as the Nazi threat of invasion grew ever stronger.*

out to sea with AA shells still bursting around its tail.'

There was an amusing sequel to this story. As he left the scene of the attack, Anthony Eden was told that the deflated balloon had been nicknamed by the local people, 'Hermann'!

If the cost of that attack had been one balloon – and they did fall from the skies in large numbers that summer, sometimes because of enemy action and on other occasions as a result of being struck by electric storms, to which they were also very vulnerable – then at least its sacrifice had prevented the Germans from damaging either people or property on the mainland.

What neither the balloons nor the Fighter Command aircraft could dispel was the growing feeling among the people as July progressed that Hitler *must* be coming soon. Radio broadcasts in English put out by German

stations boasted that invasion was imminent and that the British population was in a state of acute anxiety. 'Fear in England is indeed terrific,' the infamous Bremen station crowed. 'Men and women are trying to raise their courage by resorting to heavy drinking. Alcohol poisoning is increasing by leaps and bounds.'

A German newspaper, the *Nachtausgabe*, quoted in America, declared on 17 July: 'The whole of England is trembling on the brink of a decision. There is only a slight possibility of England offering any military resistance when our forces land.'

In a nation as devoted to gossip as the British, it is hardly surprising that rumours abounded that the Nazis were coming at any moment. Indeed, preoccupation with invasion was to be found in various forms. William Hickey, the *Daily Express*'s famous

Barrage balloons – or 'blimps' as they were popularly
known – were not only capable of bringing down
enemy aircraft that strayed too near their cables, but
their nuisance value sometimes distracted the
Luftwaffe pilots. In the photograph (above) a German
bomber on the right has narrowly missed a balloon
while fleeing from the Spitfire on his tail.

*An ill-founded fear of German poison-gas attacks had led the British Government to supply the population with gas marks; but in fact (right) there were secret plans for RAF bombers to drop mustard gas on invading German troops!*

gossip columnist, for instance, informed his readers on 3 July: 'The reader who dreamed in advance of the evacuation and fall of Paris has now dreamed that the Germans will attempt to land at the East India Dock – having crossed the sea and come up the Thames in troopships convoyed by destroyers disguised as British destroyers.'

Obviously anxious not to be labelled a rumour-monger, Hickey added: 'I merely print this as a curiosity of dream-lore: dreams are usually a confused mingling of wishes, apprehensions, memories with occasionally, so J.W. Dunne says, a flash of foreseeing. No dream, anyway, is as fantastic as the realities of this war.'

Apart from anonymous writers of letters to the press, there were also those who actually spoke out about invasion – and swiftly found themselves in court, as the following report from the *Western Daily Press* of Tuesday 16 July indicates. Headlined '74 Year Old Chatterbug', the report states: 'A man of 74, who was said to have told a neighbour that he had been

informed by a high official in Freemasonry that within a month the Swastika would be flying from the Houses of Parliament, was at Bristol yesterday sentenced to seven days in prison. The man, Alfred Joseph Richards, a compositor of Maxse Road, Knowle, Bristol, pleaded guilty to publishing by word of mouth a report of a matter concerned with the war likely to cause alarm or despondency.'

Even more likely to cause alarm and despondency was another rumour that had persisted since the declaration of war, that the German forces would use *poison gas* in any invasion. Indeed, the immediate mass distribution of the ubiquitous gas masks had been carried out to try to allay these fears, though by now they were much less in evidence than in the first few weeks of the war.

Curiously, only as recently as 1985 has it become known that the Germans never had any intention of using gas, while there *were* actually last-ditch plans made in Britain for the use of poison to repel a Nazi invasion. According to British state papers from the year 1940, declassified in February 1985, it was planned, if the Germans invaded, to drench systematically with poison large tracts of the expected beachhead from Broadstairs to Dungeness. 'Plan Y', as it was code-named, also provided for a carpet barrage of mustard gas to be laid wherever the troops might step ashore.

Perhaps most surprising of all was a scheme to use sixteen squadrons of RAF aircraft such as Lysanders, Whitleys, Blenheims and Wellingtons to fly over the Germans as they landed and spray them with mustard gas! According to the report, Britain had a stockpile of 1485 tons of the gas in 1940, and some pilots had already been receiving training in the technique of spraying the enemy using aircraft fitted with tanks of water. Still another plan was to use the Tiger Moths that had performed so valiantly in the Scarecrow Patrols to spray the Germans with a deadly insecticide containing arsenic trioxide and copper acetate.

Viewed with hindsight, it seems quite possible that only Fighter Command's triumph in the Battle of

Britain spared thousands of German soldiers from such a horrendous fate.

There were also fears abroad in July 1940 that there were traitors living in Britain who would aid the Germans once they had landed. Again, while such stories were repeated despite all the Government's efforts to stop idle tongues by way of official directives and poster campaigns, the facts such as they are did not emerge until as recently as 1986.

The release of papers, this time from the Home Office, revealed that a high-ranking officer, General Claude Liardet, had warned the Home Secretary that he had reason to believe there were people in the most vulnerable part of England, Kent, who would do all in their power to help the Nazis. 'I have British subjects in my area who are disloyal in thought,' he maintained, 'and one day, when hostile action takes place, they will be disloyal in deed.' (See the full story 'Kent traitors fear in 1940' and the interesting response it produced from another senior officer, reprinted in this chapter.)

Nor were such fears confined to Kent. Near to where I live on the borders of Suffolk and Essex, it has recently been disclosed that in the village of Dedham, near Britain's prestigious 'oldest recorded town', Colchester, there was a 'cell' of German sympathisers who even had their own appointed 'gauleiter' ready to take command of the district once the invasion of Britain had been successfully achieved! According to a local resident, when these facts were discovered by three Dedham men they determined that should the Germans land, this 'cell' and its leader would be 'immediately eliminated'.

There was, however, one amusing rumour that flourished briefly in that July – and which was just as briskly dispelled. This story maintained that Hitler had secretly flown to England to make a personal, on-the-spot 'recce' for invasion! Repeated in a number of big-city pubs, it was actually a wholly fictitious story which had originated in a novel published in the second week of July entitled *The Flying Visit* and written by Peter Fleming, the travel writer, novelist and older brother of Ian Fleming, creator of the world's most famous secret agent, James Bond.

It is perhaps understandable in a country anxious for news that the book's plot should have inspired idle chatter, for it was widely advertised and reviewed. Though *why* this should have garlanded it with the ring of truth is still a mystery! The review from *The Times* of 20 July will perhaps best explain the novel and intimate why it generated such tittle-tattle.

'The most topical of the new books,' the paper's reviewer wrote, 'is *The Flying Visit* in which Mr Peter Fleming plays with the fancy that Hitler once came to England – not by invasion but accident. It is an idea full

of possibilities, since Hitler must be human enough to feel some curiosity about a land that means so much to him. . . . Therefore, he shows him to be quite mystified by the common man, picking his way over unfamiliar country in the blackout. He shows him, rather pathetically, in fact, making gestures with no one to applaud.

'Apart from the notion of a Hitler shorn of his "Yes Men", the humour of the book is chiefly in the Government's embarrassment at finding the arch enemy in their midst. How can one expect America and other sympathetic friends to believe the news when Germany itself has never noticed its loss?'

In fact, of course, Hitler was safely at home in Berlin, still pondering over Britain's delay in surrendering, and holding back from action in the hope that

*The novel which started a rumour that Hitler had visited England! The cartoonist David Low provided these two amusing sketches for Peter Fleming's book* The Flying Visit, *published in July 1940.*

Churchill would see reason. He was, though, planning a kind of 'invasion' on the night that a BBC announcer all unknowingly made a fairly large number of listeners in Britain believe that the real thing was actually just about to happen. Shortly after midnight on 24 July, the announcer, Frank Phillips, concluded the evening's broadcasting with the cheery words, 'Goodnight everybody – *and good luck.*'

To those used to the strict impersonality of BBC announcers, it sounded very much as if Phillips was 'in the know', that he was somehow privy to events of great moment. And what was more on people's minds at that moment than invasion?

As it transpired, what *did* drop from the skies shortly afterwards was something really quite different.

# THE LAND WE DEFEND

'Catch me washing a German's pants – not likely!' Thus an indignant housewife who had been reading an account of the famous conversation manual designed for the use of Germans landing in this country – the manual that contains that immortal instruction: 'Quickly, clergyman, hand over the cash-box!' The suggestion that good British housewives should be made to wash the invaders' underclothes was too much of a good thing. The line had to be drawn somewhere and the housewife can hardly be blamed for drawing it at the clothes line. 'Let one of 'em come down this street,' she went on, 'and I'll show 'im!' What the unwelcome visitor was going to be shown can only be conjectured. All one can say definitely is that, given anything like equal terms and machine guns apart, one might very well put one's money on the housewife. She may not know much about the background of the war; and her views on the composition of the Government may not be orthodox. But let an unwanted foreigner step into her front garden and she will not be at a loss.

We are, it is said, an unimaginative and easy-going people, tending sometimes to shrug our shoulders not at the suffering of others but at the dangers that others are facing. 'Bad luck for those poor devils,' we say. 'Bet they wish they were an island, like us, and had got a Navy.' And as to that, never in all our long history have the people of these islands held their sailors in greater admiration or affection. Yet by the time these words appear it may be that the Nazi troopers will have come among us, brought over by some ingenious device that even our Navy and our splendid Air Force will not have been able wholly to frustrate. We may in fact be encountering Germans on the doorstep. We have been told, of course, that this is a war not so much of territorial frontiers as of the frontiers of the mind. And that is true. What we defend in this island is the right of all men to live the kind of lives they want to live, instead of having to live them under the baleful gaze of Himmler and his spies. Our cause is that of all mankind, and in that sense the battle of England will be the battle of the world. But abstractions to most of us need interpretation; and in this case the interpretation will not, we suspect, be very far to seek. The frontiers of the mind coincide, so far as the greater part of Europe is concerned, with the coastline of the British Isles. And those familiar features of our land which are the outward symbols of all that we are fighting for – the village church where we are free to worship, the school where our children are taught the best that is in us to teach, the assembly hall where a man can speak his mind – these well-known sights may themselves become the centre of the battle. For nearly a thousand years wars against the foreigner have meant to us battles waged abroad or on the sea; and those who have fought have done so knowing that their own country was inviolate and that when they came back it would greet them with a smiling, undisfigured landscape. But now that is changed, and we are face to face with ugly possibilities. At any moment the Philistines may be upon us.

Leader Column
*The Listener*, 11 July 1940

A widely distributed Ministry of Information leaflet to steel the resolve of the British nation.

# Kent traitors fear in 1940

A wartime general warned the Home Secretary and police in 1940 that there were traitors in Kent who would do all they could to assist the Germans.

In Home Office papers released yesterday, General Claude Liardet is quoted as saying; 'I have British subjects in my area who are disloyal in thought and one day, when hostile action takes place, they will be disloyal in deed.

'I am no alarmist, very far from it, but I know that there are a certain number of people in Kent with political views in line with Adolf Hitler and will do all they can to assist him when the opportunity arises.

'From a military operational point of view, they are a greater danger than aliens.'

The papers gave details of how the Government dealt with pro-Nazi sympathisers and foreign nationals interned in the United Kingdom.

General Liardet, who was in command of the Kent area in 1940, emphasised that the people he feared were mainly educated, knew exactly how far they could go 'and give me and the police no peg to hang our hats on'.

They had publicly expressed pro-Nazi and Fascist views, he said. At that time, 6 June 1940, 337,000 troops had just been evacuated from Dunkirk, and rumours abounded that there were German parachutists and fifth columnists in the countryside. Security chiefs had warned of parachutists, who spoke perfect English, spreading alarm and confusion.

The general told the chief constable of Kent of his fears of fifth columnists. He said: 'It is a peculiar form of British madness to allow any persons of doubtful loyalty to reside in an area which is geographically, under modern conditions of war, a dangerous area.'

He asked for them to be removed from the area, but the Home Office said there was no power to remove or intern people except in individual cases, when they could be detained under Defence Regulation 18B.

The Home Office's decision angered the general, who described it as 'wretchedly supine and weak'.

*The Times*, 11 and 18 February 1986

# Traitors in 1940

*From Brigadier B. Chichester-Cooke*

Sir, It would be sad if your report today (February 11) lent credence to the idea that Kent was traitor-ridden in 1940. If memory serves me right, Claude Liardet did not command Kent, but the 56th (London TA) Division, which was quartered at that time in East Kent.

He was one of a small group of senior officers who were convinced that Germany had, over the years, built up in Britain a highly trained organisation of traitors, saboteurs, and ill-disposed persons who, on the word, would shoot up the air defence personnel and disable their equipment, and immobilise and contain the ground defences, to allow the unopposed landing of fleets of tanks at Folkestone to romp up the A2 to London in two hours, instead of a wasteful frontal attack.

At the time I was commanding a fair slice of the AA defences in Biggin Hill sector with detachments all over Kent and I well remember Claude sending the late Brigadier Guy Portman to persuade me to join in the hunt for 'these vermin'.

It was my contrary view that at that moment every able-bodied person in Kent had embraced the newly formed Local Defence Volunteers and, with enormous zeal, armed with an armband and a 12-bore and whipped up by all this 'traitor' talk, was making movement, especially at night, almost impossible.

I never discovered who it was that Claude wanted to lock up, but I suspect it included some of the farmers and landowners who attacked him strongly because his troops entered their lands and buildings searching for illicit rendezvous or arms caches, trampling down crops and letting out livestock.

If there were any pro-enemy incidents, I cannot find anyone who has heard about them. In contrast, the sheep farmers of Kent and the Romney Marsh readily allowed millions of sheep to be removed to deny an invading force a meat supply. It broke their hearts and ruined their flocks as well as many of themselves. But they did it.

Yours faithfully,
B. CHICHESTER-COOKE,
Hammond Place,
Upnor,
Rochester,
Kent.
February 11.

*Hitler's leaflet 'A Last Appeal to Reason', dropped by
his bombers over England, provoked amusement
rather than anxiety among the population.*

# —5—

# 'ENGLAND – WE ARE COMING!'

The steady drone of aircraft engines was heard across the counties of Hampshire and Somerset during the night of Thursday 1 August, waking many people from their uneasy sleep. Though aircraft going overhead was nothing really new to the men and women of southern England, those who particularly remember this first night of what was to prove a crucial month in the war later recalled that there was something very *ominous* about the sound. And those who peered blearily out through their blacked-out windows, or listened from the comfort of their beds to the sound, were in no doubt that the aircraft were coming from the south and therefore must be the enemy.

Some folk waited nervously for any indication that the planes might be getting lower and perhaps going to land, while others strained their ears for the sound of British interceptors. But neither happened, and nor did the sirens set up their accustomed unearthly wail. Then, in a while, the droning passed away completely.

After a few minutes more, however, *something* began to fall from out of the darkness.

Fewer people than might be expected actually saw what fell from the bomb bays of the German raiders – for such they were – because there was little to hear and most were already thankfully asleep again. That discovery was to come in the morning when dawn broke over the two counties. For lying everywhere, on roads, across fields, in gardens and even on rooftops, was a trail of pieces of paper that had fallen like confetti across the countryside.

It had not been the long-expected parachutists or bombs that the planes had scattered, but thousands upon thousands of leaflets, each one bearing the headline in inches-high type: A LAST APPEAL TO REASON by ADOLF HITLER. And as the folk of Hampshire and Somerset emerged sleepily from their homes on that bright summer morning, there before them lay the first Nazi attempt at pamphleteering: a message from Hitler to the people of England to lay down their arms.

The leaflets, printed in green and yellow, were enough of a novelty to be eagerly picked up and read. But soon one reader after another was chuckling with mirth and screwing up the paper, or else showing it to his neighbour. The reason for this amusement is not hard to imagine – the people had all heard or read the Fuehrer's message before, and as it hadn't made much of an impression *then* why should it now?

The leaflet was, in fact, a reprint of the speech he had delivered at the Reichstag as long ago as 19 July, and it had been widely quoted in the British press and on the radio. In essence the message was as follows.

'In this hour I feel it to be my duty before my own conscience to appeal once more to reason and common sense, to Great Britain as much as elsewhere. I consider myself in a position to make this appeal since I am not the vanquished seeking favours, but the victor speaking in the name of reason. I can see no reason why this war must go on. I am grieved to think of the sacrifices which it will claim. I should like to avert them also for my own people.'

And turning to those he saw as the stumbling block to this appeal, the British Government, he went on: 'Possibly Mr Churchill will again brush aside this statement of mine by saying it is merely born of fear. In that case I have relieved my conscience with regard to the things to come. Mr Churchill ought for once to believe me when I say that a great Empire will be destroyed – an Empire which it was never my intention to destroy or even harm.

'I do, however, realise that this struggle, if it continues, can end only with the complete annihilation of one or other of the two adversaries. Mr Churchill may believe that this will be Germany: *I* know it will be Britain!'

Across the two counties – and much of southern

The Junkers JU87s, or 'Stuka Bombers', which were used by the Luftwaffe to drop many thousands of leaflets across England in the summer of 1940. They were also capable of carrying a single deadly 1100 lb bomb. The raider nearest the camera has evidently been badly damaged by Fighter Command.

England and Wales where bombers also dropped the leaflets in succeeding nights – the reaction to this pamphlet raid was well summed up by an Air Raid Warden. In a report in the *Daily Mirror* the man was described as having staggered into his command post with a bundle under his arm and remarked. 'Why take all this trouble to tell us something we already *know*?' According to the *Mirror*, 'Hot news!' had been the fairly general sarcastic comment about the leaflet.

Indeed, just how light-heartedly the people took the 'raid' once they knew what it was all about can be judged from a report in the *Daily Express* which reported how the leaflets had been used to perpetrate a practical joke. 'In one country district,' the paper stated, 'when a newsagent left his house to start out on his newspaper round he found a little pile of the leaflets on his shop door step. Needless to say they were not redistributed!'

*The Times*, on Saturday 3 August, also reported how one ingenious young woman had found a way of turning the leaflets to good use. 'In the south-west of England,' the paper said, 'many of the leaflets have been the means of raising funds for the Red Cross. A farmer has been charging sixpence to sightseers who wanted to look at a bomb crater in his fields – giving the money to the Red Cross – and this gave a young woman in the same area an idea for doing the same thing with the leaflets.

'Within a short space of time,' the paper added gleefully, 'she had collected over £2 in return for these souvenirs!' (As a point of interest, *The Times* also noted in its columns that the Germans seemed to have picked a singularly inappropriate date for their pamphleteering, for 1 August 1940 marked the 200th anniversary of the first performance of that most jingoistic of British tunes, 'Rule Britannia', composed by Dr T. Arne, which had been sung to honour the accession of George I on the same date in 1740!)

Hitler had surely never imagined that his pamphlet would be treated as a mere souvenir – and with such contempt – for there is evidence that he held the British people in high esteem and for a time *did* want to negotiate a settlement with the Government to prevent a bloodbath between the two peoples he admired.

It is also true that at the very moment when England was most at his mercy following the retreat from France, Hitler was ignoring the advice of his army generals to storm the little island across the Channel. Indeed, on a triumphant visit to France, Hitler told Field Marshal von Runstedt in a manner that brooked no argument, 'I will make peace with England and offer her an alliance. Germany will dominate Europe, and England the world outside.'

A few days later, on 18 June, the Fuehrer was expressing these same sentiments just as forcefully in Berlin to the Italian Foreign Minister, Count Ciano, who wrote in his diary, 'Hitler makes many reservations on the desirability of demolishing the British Empire, which he considers even today to be an important factor in world equilibrium. Hitler is now the gambler who has made a big scoop and would like to get up from the table risking nothing more.'

A month later, on 19 July, at the ceremony to install Goering as the first Reichsmarschall, Hitler, apparently unaware or unperturbed at the frenzied aircraft building going on in England, offered the olive branch to the British Government once again, in the speech later reprinted in the notorious pamphlets.

As before, Count Ciano was on hand to record the effect on the Fuehrer of another rebuff. 'I believe his desire for peace is sincere,' the Italian minister confided to his diary. 'In fact, late in the evening, when the first cold British reactions to the speech arrived, a sense of disappointment spread among the Germans.'

Nevertheless, the German propaganda machine was ordered to work overtime to convince the British people they should make Churchill and his Cabinet change their minds. Prominent in this campaign were the strident tones of 'Lord Haw-Haw', the English traitor William Joyce in Berlin. 'Churchill means hunger and war!' a statement read in English over German radio thundered. 'When the capitalists set out to make this bloody war, who did they call upon to fight it for them? The working class, of course!'

English listeners, aware of how men and women from all backgrounds had hurried forward to offer themselves for the Services, laughed at such nonsense – as they also did at Radio Bremen's hysterical claim that when things got really bad in England there would be an uprising among the starving working classes and soldiers would be ordered to fire on them to restore order. 'You, the men in arms, will be ordered to shoot your friends, your brothers, even your own sisters!' the announcer said.

As if vainly hoping such absurd stories might cause the British to see his idea of reason, Hitler was still refusing to sanction an invasion as the month drew to a close. But following the formal rejection, Hitler then told Goering on 30 July to be ready to begin 'the great air battle against England' at twelve hours' notice.

(overleaf) *'How to Meet the Threat of Invasion'* – a special feature in the Illustrated London News *to prepare the people of Britain for German landings.*

# MEETING THE THREAT OF AIR-BORNE INVASION IN BRITAIN:

DRAWN BY OUR SPECIAL

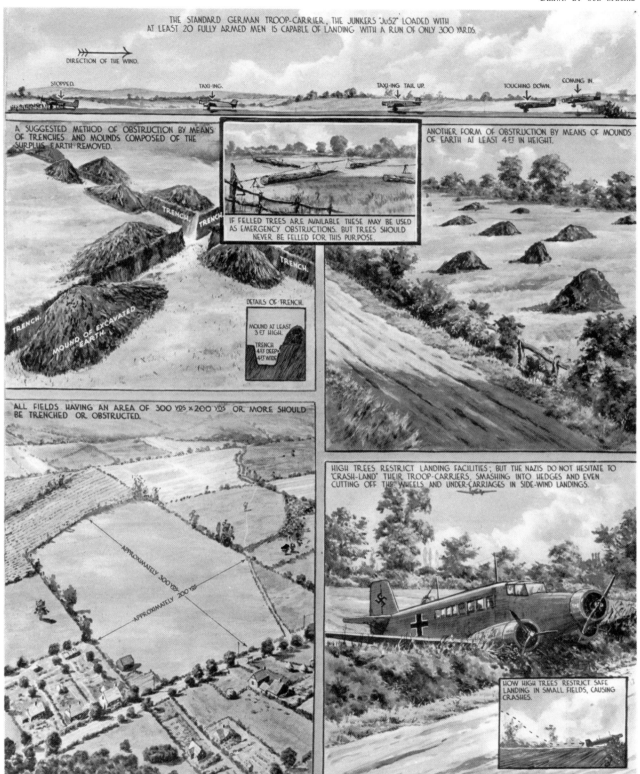

THE STANDARD GERMAN TROOP-CARRIER, THE JUNKERS "Ju52" LOADED WITH AT LEAST 20 FULLY ARMED MEN IS CAPABLE OF LANDING WITH A RUN OF ONLY 300 YARDS.

DIRECTION OF THE WIND.

STOPPED. TAXI-ING. TAXI-ING TAIL UP. TOUCHING DOWN. COMING IN

A SUGGESTED METHOD OF OBSTRUCTION BY MEANS OF TRENCHES AND MOUNDS COMPOSED OF THE SURPLUS EARTH REMOVED.

TRENCH. TRENCH. TRENCH. TRENCH. MOUND OF EXCAVATED EARTH

IF FELLED TREES ARE AVAILABLE THESE MAY BE USED AS EMERGENCY OBSTRUCTIONS, BUT TREES SHOULD NEVER BE FELLED FOR THIS PURPOSE.

ANOTHER FORM OF OBSTRUCTION BY MEANS OF MOUNDS OF EARTH AT LEAST 4 FT IN HEIGHT.

DETAILS OF TRENCH.
MOUND AT LEAST 3 FT HIGH.
TRENCH 4 FT DEEP 4 FT WIDE.

ALL FIELDS HAVING AN AREA OF 300 YDS × 200 YDS OR MORE SHOULD BE TRENCHED OR OBSTRUCTED.

APPROXIMATELY 300 YDS
APPROXIMATELY 200 YDS

HIGH TREES RESTRICT LANDING FACILITIES; BUT THE NAZIS DO NOT HESITATE TO "CRASH-LAND" THEIR TROOP-CARRIERS, SMASHING INTO HEDGES AND EVEN CUTTING OFF THE WHEELS AND UNDER-CARRIAGES IN SIDE-WIND LANDINGS.

HOW HIGH TREES RESTRICT SAFE LANDING IN SMALL FIELDS, CAUSING CRASHES.

## NAZI TROOP-CARRIERS, WHICH PLAYED A VITAL PART IN THE INVASION OF NORWAY AND HOLLAND, CAN CRASH-LAND
### BY WHICH THEY CAN BE HINDERED

In the light of the aerial invasions which have so largely brought about the submissions successively of Poland, Norway, Holland and Belgium, the menace of the troop-carrying aeroplane is a very real one to Britain. Various counter-measures are possible which may have the effect of thwarting the enemy's plans in this direction, one being to obstruct open country where troop-carriers could land, and also arterial roads and, finally, rivers so that the big aircraft, carrying their human loads of enemy soldiers, will be unable to alight without crashing. On these pages we illustrate various means of obstructing such fields as

might offer troop-carriers chances of emergency landings. Britain, with its wealth of trees and ubiquitous hedges, provides many more natural obstacles than have been offered by the countries successively invaded by the Nazis. On the other hand, in the ruthless determination of the German High Command to carry out its will, great risks are taken by the pilots of the troop-carriers and many "crash" landings have been reported, when aircraft were brought down in very restricted areas and smashed in ditches. Some even were brought down in side-winds, and had their under-carriages wrenched off, while others were landed

# SUGGESTED MEASURES FOR FOILING NAZI TROOP-CARRIERS.

Artist G. H. Davis.

IN RELATIVELY SMALL SPACES. THESE DRAWINGS SHOW THEIR CAPABILITIES, AND SUGGEST A NUMBER OF WAYS OR STOPPED IN THIS COUNTRY.

down-wind and bumped and bounced over ploughed fields and similar rough surfaces, oftentimes throwing their inmates in a heap and breaking arms and legs. Yet as long as a certain percentage of the men reached the invaded soil unscathed the demands of the Nazi generals were satisfied. Such desperate tactics must, of course, also be anticipated in any attempted invasion of our own island. Everywhere over the English countryside—surpassingly beautiful just now in the full tide of summer—are open spaces, and each area of over two hundred square yards is a potential landing-field for Nazi troop-carriers, which,

with the use of air-brakes, can reduce their run on alighting to three hundred yards and get off again in only a little more space after the troops have left them. The need therefore appears to be vital to place obstructions in the way of such possible landings, either through trenching or the raising of effective obstacles, and it is gratifying to learn that steps are already being taken to this end. In many areas, particularly around Greater London, the defence of open spaces was recently stated to be complete. Soldiers have been ploughing up certain areas and trenches have been dug.

*Czech pilots preparing to join in the Battle of Britain at
the Fighter Command base at Cosford.*

(left) *A best-selling paperback rushed out in the summer of 1940 to combat the waves of German propaganda.* (right) *One advertiser at least managed to make a little humorous capital out of the invasion scare!*

waiting near their machines at a fighter station somewhere in England. They are all ready to meet German raiders.' Just *how* ready was to be shown in the next few vital weeks.

While Dowding and his 'Chicks' waited, the activity across the Channel continued as Goering drew up his plans. Kesselring and Sperrle were to concentrate their two Luftflotte units on attacking objectives in the south of England for the first few days, then General Stumpff's Luftflotte 5 would follow up with attacks on the Midlands and north. The brash Reichsmarschall spoke confidently of breaking Britain's southern air defences in four days and of destroying the RAF itself within four weeks.

But as the pilots and people of Britain awaited the Luftwaffe, the character of the nation continued to assert itself in moments of typical eccentricity. In London, for example, at Lord's, the RAF took advan-

But it seemed that Goering, too, had come to believe his Fuehrer's claim that the English would sue for peace, and he was undoubtedly far from fully prepared to act on such a directive. Hastily, on 1 August, he roused his lieutenants Kesselring, Sperrle and Stumpff and ordered them to prepare their air armadas for operation *Adler Tag* ('Eagle Day').

In Britain, by contrast, the population was enjoying the traditional Bank Holiday weekend – war or no war – and *The Times* newspaper felt confident enough that the nation had made excellent use of its breathing space and was ready for any eventuality to print a happy photograph showing a group of pilots lounging on the grass in front of their aircraft. 'All Ready,' read the caption underneath. 'Cheerful pilots of Hurricanes

.tage of the lull to play a game of cricket against the London Fire Service, while shoppers suddenly found a plentiful supply of bananas had somehow found their way to the beleaguered nation!

In Parliament there were happier faces than usual when the Chancellor of the Exchequer announced that he was to increase the pay of Servicemen. 'I have come to the conclusion,' he said, 'that in all the circumstances, alleviation is warranted, and it is proposed, therefore, to make an increase in pay of sixpence a day to warrant officers, non-commissioned officers and men.' (According to *Hansard*, this speech was greeted with 'cheers from the House'.)

But to those at home who might have time on their hands, the Government issued a new order for lofts and attics to be cleared 'at once'. This was as a precaution against fires being caused by falling incendiary bombs. The Minister of Home Security instructed householders in urban areas to clear their lofts of all movable articles – though lofts or attics where there was a fixed staircase or where they were used or furnished for living in were excluded!

In the press, the story which excited the most attention appeared on Friday 2 August and concerned the exploits of an unnamed Fighter Command pilot who had flown to France, passed over a village he had known in peace-time, and, seeing a group of German troops goose-stepping across the square, angrily sprayed them with machine-gun fire. It was a yarn almost straight from the pages of a novel, and whatever the man's commanding officer may have felt, his

*America enters the Battle of Britain. Hardly was the battle won than British cinema audiences were treated to the sight of future President Ronald Reagan playing an American pilot who joined the RAF in the movie* International Squadron *(1941) and almost single-handedly won the day! The badge of the Eagle Squadron of US pilots who were attached to the RAF was worn with considerable bravery and skill by many unsung heroes from across the Atlantic.*

exploit caused many a smile over breakfast tables that Friday morning.

The pilot gave an account of his flight to some colleagues on his return. 'I was flying solo high over German-occupied France,' he said, 'and decided to come down through the clouds to have a look round. I found myself only about 70 feet from the ground and approaching a village I had visited before the war. Following the straight road leading to the village I recognised the church on the left-hand side, the odd cluster of cottages, and the *estaminets*. The town hall in the square was still standing.

'Then I saw two lines of German soldiers in the square, goose-stepping as hard as they could go. It seemed sacrilege to me as I had known the village in happier times. So I edged my machine down a bit, and when they came in range I pressed the firing button. The Germans went down like a pack of cards.

'Then I swung round and came back to see what the result was. Those who had not been hit were running

*A German propaganda poster of the summer of 1940.*

for shelter, but most of them were lying where they had fallen. They obviously thought that the low clouds would keep off any aircraft, and were doing a bit of goose-stepping to annoy the local inhabitants.'

Although readers of the papers had no way of knowing it, that poor visibility which had aided the pilot was also to influence the German plans to attack Britain. For the hot, sunny month of July was followed by a damp and misty early August. Under the cover of this, on 5 August, the first convoy since 23 July was able to sail safely up the Channel from Falmouth to the Thames Estuary without attack from enemy aircraft.

Tuesday 6 August brought the report of the first ever battle between two float planes over the Channel. A Short Sunderland of the Royal Australian Flying Squadron flying with Coastal Command had encountered a Dornier 18 obviously on a scouting mission and, coming up on the German unawares, emptied an almost complete burst of machine-gun fire into the aircraft.

At this, the German pilot had turned and come back at the Sunderland head on. But by clever manoeuvring, the young Melbourne flight lieutenant at the controls managed to avoid serious damage beyond some bullet-holes in his craft's upper structure, and had then brought his own guns into play to fire another round. The Dornier dived to sea level – according to the report – where it was attacked again, and was last seen limping into a cloud bank. The Australian pilot searched the area for twenty minutes without discovering any sign of the enemy, who he was convinced had fallen into the sea.

Apart from this Australian, there were quite a number of other pilots from abroad who had rushed to augment the RAF's depleted ranks and were now beginning to see action over England. Among them were men who had fled from the overrun countries of Europe such as France, Poland and Czechoslovakia and were now rubbing shoulders with pilots from the British Commonwealth as well as the first of what was to prove a steady stream of Americans.

It was also on 6 August that British newspapers first told the public that there were Americans in the RAF – in the following story of an air battle over the Channel.

'One of the Spitfire pilots was a 27-year-old American who just seven weeks ago was showing young Americans how to fly at Larado airfield in Texas near the Mexican border,' said an account in *The Times*. 'He chased two Messerschmitts and hit one, and was himself attacked by the other enemy fighter. He got back safely with the squadron, but his Spitfire was rendered temporarily unserviceable. The fuselage was peppered with tiny holes and one of the cables inside was completely severed. "The fight was great," he said

## Beware The "Air-Brained"

"AIR - BRAINED," nothing - will - happen - to - me folks who walked the streets of a coast town yesterday after the sirens had given warning of an air raid, are condemned by the Ministry of Home Security.

It is pointed out that they were not brave, but merely stupid. They were not defying the Nazis, but playing into their hands.

Sensible people who take cover when warned to do so are asked to try and influence those foolish persons. They will be doing a public service.

afterwards.'

On Thursday 8 August a Polish pilot in a Hurricane squadron was reported to have taken part in his first battle over the Channel. After the action – and with the assistance of colleagues who translated his words – the man described what happened when he encountered a formation of Junker 87s supported by Heinkel 113 fighters.

'I was attacked by three Heinkel 113s who seemed to be working to a plan. One was flying alone, with the other two as a pair. If you attack the pair, the single one tries to get on your tail. I tackled the single 113 and watched it go down smoking, though I did not see the final crash. The other two flew off.'

According to the report, the Polish pilot was credited with his first official 'kill', a Messerschmitt 109, in another engagement he took part in later that same day.

August 8 was, in fact, a significant day for Fighter Command over the Channel where it defended the first major west-bound convoy from the Thames Estuary.

Entering the Straits of Dover at first light, the ships were set upon by the Luftwaffe and there followed what proved to be the first dawn-to-dusk German offensive – Kesselring and Sperrle putting several hundred bombers and fighters into the attack, which in turn meant a large number of RAF pilots taking part in as many as five operations during the day. By the end of the day the tally of losses stood at 28 Luftwaffe aircraft to 19 British fighters. In the Channel, at least seven ships had been sunk.

Beginning that same day, too, the Germans initiated a veritable barrage of propaganda predicting the impending doom of Britain. 'England, we are coming!' screamed the Nazi press and radio.

The front page of the *Hamburger Fremdenblatt*, the organ of the German Foreign Office, declared unequivocally: 'An attack by the mighty forces of Germany will be made on Britain in the near future!' And the report went on: 'Napoleon, in spite of all the preparations he had made, flinched at the last moment from making the attempt to conquer the island. But under the inspired hand of Adolf Hitler, who is the real Holy Ghost, the modern weapons the Reich possesses can, and quickly will, put an end to the insularity of Britain. England still thinks in terms of the past. The fate of the British people is being staked on a last trump card – namely, that the poor old-fashioned degenerate British Isles can defy our bombers, submarines, E-Boats and our batteries set up on the Channel coast, because Britain, in spite of all, is an island. The destruction of this illusion is about to be undertaken.'

The theme was also front-page news in the *Schwartz Corps*, the organ of Hitler's Guards, which under a headline 'England We Are Coming' stated: 'Not only the eleventh, but also the twelfth hour has passed and the clock is now striking one. In rejecting the appeal to the British people, we now know that Churchill and his egotistical comrades will fall not by their own laws but by the laws which we shall have fought with. The time of waiting is over. We are coming!'

The *Nachtausgabe* was another paper to run a report, headlined 'The Germans Are Coming!', which claimed, 'England realises the bitter truth – landing cannot be prevented.' Its conclusions, it said, were based on alleged expressions of opinion given by British military experts in the British press!

The researcher will look in vain through the pages of all British newspapers and magazines from those early August days for *any* such expressions of opinion – but what can be found instead is every indication of a resolute nation with its back to the wall ready to fight and withstand anything the German aerial bombardment might bring.

Hitler had, in fact, already set 10 August for *Adler Tag*: the day when the might of the German Luftwaffe was to begin crushing Britain. The night before, however, an incident occurred on the Sussex coast which seems in retrospect a perfect expression of the courage and concern for humanity which was at the heart of the British stance against Nazi Germany. It concerned an English Spitfire pilot who gave up his own life after an aerial fight rather than allow his crashing plane to hit a coastal town. Until recently, the names of both the man and the place his brave action spared have remained unknown – but through my researches for this book I have been able to solve at least one part of the mystery.

The *Daily Telegraph*'s report of the incident read: 'Smoke and flames were streaming from the tail of the Spitfire as the pilot straightened out after a dive which had taken him towards a south-east coastal town. The plane skimmed the roofs of houses, losing height all the time, and it seemed that it must crash into the centre of the town. With great skill he turned the machine from its course and several seconds later it crashed into the sea not more than fifty yards from the water's edge.

'Everyone who saw the machine falling expected the pilot to bale out,' the report added. 'Had he done so the plane would have crashed on to some houses. It burnt itself out on the surface of the water within a few minutes. Motor launches hurried to the spot, but found only floating wreckage.'

My enquiries have established that the town the brave pilot so narrowly missed was Worthing. And by one of those strange twists of fate, even if the plane had crashed on to the beach (which it also narrowly missed), no lives would have been lost. For in an emergency meeting just the previous night, Worthing Town Council had decided to place a total ban on bathing along the whole of the sea front.

WHEN A MESSERSCHMITT
THROWS UP THE SPONGE.

A BAIL-OUT BY AN OPPONENT
IS NOW TAKEN AS A VICTORY —
A GERMAN PILOT WHEN
VANQUISHED HAS TO TURN
HIS FIGHTER UPSIDE DOWN SO
THAT HE CAN DROP HEAD FIRST
OUT OF THE NARROW COCKPIT.

*The British traitor turned German broadcaster, 'Lord Haw-Haw', was a favourite butt of cartoonists such as John G. Walter who contributed this example to* Punch, *10 July 1940.*

" *I heard a rumour that Lord Haw Haw has given the inside story about Mrs. Robinson and the Women's Institute Prize Cake Competition.*"

## NAZI TALES

### J.B. Priestley on German Propaganda

I have talked a good deal to you lately on the radio about Nazi propaganda in its wider, more sinister and more successful aspects, showing how the Nazis go from country to country encouraging opposition in each country to any party that is opposed to them, pretending to be friends of the rich in one place and friends of the poor in another, changing their colour whenever it should be necessary, and above all encouraging everywhere those men whom they recognise to be of the same psychological type as themselves, men who will do anything for power. In this kind of propaganda, which has always been backed by plenty of hard cash, the Nazis have been very successful. But when we come to a more topical and intimate type of propaganda, we notice at once that they are far less successful, almost dead failures. And for a very good reason. The Nazis at home are by this time used to dealing with an exceptionally credulous and foolish public, who almost ask to be taken away from reality – and, whether they ask for it or not, *are* taken away from reality and told ridiculous fairy tales. We shouldn't be surprised that the German people are now like that, for the whole aim of Nazi education, if it can fairly be called education, is to abolish the least glimmer of any critical intelligence, and the doubters and scoffers, who refused to be hoodwinked, have either been sent into exile, taken to concentration camps, or bullied into silence. The rest of their public simply asks to be taken in, to be doped with lies and nonsense, to live in a mental Cloud Cuckoodom. Having this silly and easy public to handle at home, the Nazi propagandists who deal with the topical and more intimate stuff are simply too careless and slapdash in their propaganda of this sort for abroad – with the not unpleasant result that some of the best laughs we get come from the labours of these solemn idiots. For example, this week they have been telling the world about what is happening in London.

Nothing could be more fantastic than their accounts of this London that they have invented. In this London of theirs, for instance, we are told that 'people are providing themselves with private machine-gun nests'. I'd like to see the face of an officer of our Royal Ordnance Corps if a private citizen came to him and asked for armaments for a private machine-gun nest. But that is only the beginning. They can do much better than that. 'There are,' they tell us, 'riots in London every night, and it is getting impossible to live in town.' Where these nightly riots are and who joins in them, we aren't told; but I am out nearly every night and return home at all hours, and I have yet to see anything that looked remotely like a riot. Perhaps their spies listen to conversations they don't understand, and hearing one theatrical manager telling another that his new musical show is a riot they jump to the conclusion that the populace must be rioting.

And here's a beauty, I think my favourite: 'The fear of German planes is terrific. One of the best proofs of this is that the Jews are having their hair dyed and their noses straightened.' It's a shame to spoil that exquisite invention even by commenting on it. Let's just leave it, and imagine that Oxford Street and Regent Street and Piccadilly and Bond Street and the Strand are now filled with shops in which Jews are having their hair dyed and their noses straightened. The whole West End is crowded with people who have bright golden hair and very straight noses. The rest of us, not being busy with hair-dyeing and nose-straightening, have nothing else to do but to suffer from this terrific fear of German planes. You can't hear yourself speak in the streets for the chattering of teeth and the knocking of knees. Everybody is so terrified in London that you see the people every night crowding into restaurants and eating and drinking and laughing and dancing, pushing their way into theatres and film shows, hiding themselves in ice skating and roller skating rinks, at whist drives or greyhound racing, listening to music or watching the ballet, and at the week-end going to tennis courts and golf links. I tell you, the panic is awful. At least, that's how it looks from Berlin. Here in London it isn't quite so obvious. I was talking this afternoon to a young American journalist, who had landed here, paying us his first visit, only a week or two ago. *He* told me, though of course he couldn't possibly know as much about it as these people in Berlin, that he had been staggered by the cheerful calm of the folk here, which seemed almost restful after the huge headlines and the excitement about the war in New York.

Now for the supreme effort of this week's Nazi propaganda, which is this: 'Panic in Britain is so great that millions are leaving the country.' For sheer impudence, this has never been beaten so far in the war. Consider the statement that millions – *millions* – are leaving this country. Where are they going to, these millions? And how are they going, these millions? Taking a very modest estimate of 'millions', let us say there are two million people involved. 'Now, there are only two ways of leaving this country, either by passenger plane or by ship. It would take at least 40,000 passenger planes to remove two million persons, far, far more big passenger planes than exist in the whole world. It would take a thousand first-class large liners to remove these same people by sea, far more first-class large liners than exist in the whole world. Then these millions cannot have left this island either by air or by sea, and they certainly haven't been walking away from it, so how have they gone?

BBC Radio broadcast
2 August 1940

DEALING WITH THE DIVE BOMBER AT OSTERLEY PARK

MEMBERS OF THE HOME GUARD PRACTISING RAPID RIFLE FIRE AGAINST A DIVING PLANE.

THE MODEL REPRESENTS A 50 ft. SPAN PLANE, DIVING FROM A HEIGHT OF 1500 ft. THE TIME TAKEN FOR THIS MODEL TO REACH THE BOTTOM OF ITS WIRE RUNWAY IS ROUGHLY 3 SECONDS.

WHEN IT IS WITHIN 18 INCHES OF THE GROUND IT SWOOPS UPWARDS IN A STEEP CLIMB BARELY SKIMMING THE HEADS OF THE FIRING PARTY.

THE MAXIMUM RATE OF FIRE HAS PROVED TO BE THREE ROUNDS. THAT IS, TWO AS THE MACHINE DECENDS, AND ONE AS IT SOARS UPWARDS TOWARDS THE TREE TOPS.

A MEDLEY OF BURSTING FIRE CRACKERS ARE LET LOOSE FOR SOUND EFFECTS AND TO DISCONCERT THE RIFLEMEN.

VARIOUS SHALLOW TRENCHES AFFORD A VARIETY OF FIRING POSITIONS, AND THE WHOLE CONTRIVANCE MAKES EXCELLENT PRACTICE FOR QUICK AIMING AND LOADING.

· CUNEO ·

# —6—

# THE EAGLE
# WILL *NOT* LAND!

Saturday 10 August was the day decreed by Hitler for Goering's Luftwaffe to commence *Adler Tag*. The Eagle was not only to drive the Sparrows of the RAF out of the skies, but leave the British nation helpless for invasion. All unsuspectingly, as that day dawned, many people on this side of the Channel prepared for their usual weekend pursuits: a bit of shopping, some gardening, maybe a walk or even a game of golf, tennis or cricket . . .

A day or two earlier in France, Kesselring, still feeling the warm glow from the presentation of a Field Marshal's baton from Hitler, had been happy to boast to a party of foreign journalists who visited his headquarters that the next stage of the war would be short and spectacular. He also took the opportunity to indulge in a little cloak-and-dagger mystery by suggesting he had a secret weapon up his sleeve. A correspondent of the *New York Times* wrote on 7 August: 'In the course of a tour through parts of Belgium and France, Field Marshal Kesselring told foreign journalists that Germany had ready for use against Britain secret weapons and methods of warfare 'perhaps never used before'. He would not, however, say what the weapons were or whether he meant merely there was to be a new use of old weapons. But he said that the weapons used to subdue France could not be expected to work against England, because the enemy was an island.'

More interesting than this little exercise in intrigue was the Field Marshal's answer to the question whether Britain was stronger because of Germany's delay in making a direct attack upon her. The report continued: 'The Field Marshal replied "Not significantly." He said this was because it was becoming increasingly difficult for England to obtain supplies as a result of the German attacks on British harbours. He praised the Spitfire as a fighter, but derided the Hurricane. The Field Marshal said that American airplanes were better than any Britain was producing.'

Kesselring's fellow commander of Luftflotte 3, Field Marshal Sperrle (he, too, had been awarded his baton by Hitler), was feeling equally loquacious, and issued his own statement to the world's press on 8 August. 'The German Air Force stands ready in a wide crescent stretching from Trondheim to Brest,' he said. 'In the centre at the present lies its main objective, the comparatively small island of England. There is no point on the island out of reach of our bombers. The attacks of the German Air Force will be directed against important military objectives, the centres of English industry, against harbours and docks.'

The main weapon, Sperrle said, would be the bomber, attacking in continuous waves, each protected by fighters. And as if taking a leaf from Kesselring's book of surprises – though, as we shall learn, it was more likely because the Field Marshal was unsure of precisely *what* his objectives were – he added, 'The attack will not come in the form which is anticipated in England.'

Such bravado cut little ice with Dowding, who had meticulously planned his defensive moves and carefully briefed his men. He had also been much heartened by the recent achievements of his pilots. In the previous month, while defending the convoys, the Germans had usually attacked in formations of about fifty machines. On average they had lost a dozen planes a day to the RAF's seven, the figures from 10 July to 10 August being 286 German aircraft destroyed as against 150 British fighters.

*Members of the Home Guard training to repel German dive bombers – an on-the-spot sketch by Terence Cuneo.*

An estimate of the actual numbers of aircraft each side possessed at this time makes salutary reading. The three German air groups based on the airfields in France, the Low Countries and Norway could muster 1000 long-range bombers, 702 single-seater fighters, 261 heavy fighters and 300 dive bombers. In addition there were 1000 more aircraft out of service for one reason or another. Fighter Command's total tactical strength was 720, with approximately the same number grounded temporarily or being deliberately held in reserve. The British figures had, of course, been dramatically improved by the delivery of some 500 new Hurricanes and Spitfires during the month, and it remains to the eternal credit of the unsung RAF maintenance crews on airfields across the country that rarely did the operational strength drop below 700 during the remainder of the Battle of Britain.

Fighter Command's only real shortage was, of course, fully trained fighter pilots. But where Britain had a decided advantage was when aircraft were shot down. RAF pilots brought down over their own territory might well survive, and quite often their machines, too, could be salvaged for parts. Shot-down German aircraft, on the other hand, were lost completely to the Luftwaffe, while their pilots became POWs.

On the dawn of the planned Eagle Day, another ally came to the aid of Britain – the weather. Drizzling rain and low clouds threw all the German plans into confusion and there was no other alternative for Goering but to stand down his men and machines for two days. The weather did not wholly confine Fighter Command, however, and during that weekend of 10 and 11 August the RAF carried out no fewer than three bombing raids on a little outpost of Britain – the island of Guernsey, off the west coast of France, which by then was under German occupation. The raids were instigated as a result of

between forty and fifty German bombers being reported on the island's only aerodrome at Le Bourg. The RAF pilots successfully bombed several planes left on the runways, damaged hangars and carried out low-flying attacks on the airfield's defence posts.

It was, though, at dawn on Tuesday 13 August that the long-awaited Eagle Day was finally launched by the German air forces – although the weather was once again far from ideal. A thick bank of cloud as low as 4000 feet hung over Kent and much of Sussex. Yet with cries of 'Victory by August 15th!', the German pilots roared into action across the Channel. The bombers were instructed to strike at a variety of targets including harbours, factories and RAF bases, while the fighters were to lure their opposite numbers into the air and destroy them. Viewed with hindsight, it was a plan that was simply not specific enough in its objectives to be certain of success against a well-organised defence.

*'Britain on Top' was the patriotic caption on this Ministry of Information official photograph released on 20 August.*

As leading historian Basil Collier has written: 'It seems clear that the explanation of their apparently random choice of targets was that Goering wanted to do too much in too short a time. Notoriously little interested in the invasion plans of the other Services because he thought that they would never be put into effect, he believed that, by attacking a wide range of targets, the Luftwaffe could, at one and the same time, not only destroy Dowding's squadrons in the air but cause such havoc on the ground that the country would be brought to the verge of surrender, or beyond it, by the time the German Army was ready to go ashore.'

In any event, a formation of eighty bombers from Luftflotte 2 were the first over England before breakfast-time that Tuesday morning – to be met at once by a Spitfire squadron over the Thames Estuary; while 60 miles to the west, two groups of bombers from Luftflotte 3 with a fighter escort crossed the Sussex coast to find themselves within the gun sights of waiting Hurricanes. The effectiveness of Fighter Command's radar system had in no way been hampered by the poor visibility.

A pilot who was among the first to answer the call to 'scramble' on 13 August later gave a vivid eye-witness account of this opening encounter. Like so many others quoted in the press at this time, his name is unknown.

'My flight took off shortly after 6.30 with orders to patrol the Channel south of the Isle of Wight. The first thing we came across were two formations of bombers, Junkers 87. We went straight at them. We got at a few of the bombers and then got mixed up with their escorting Messerschmitts. I remember seeing two of them about a quarter of a mile away coming straight at me at 16,000 feet.

'Suddenly, for no apparent reason, one of them did a half roll and went straight down. I followed, and though I did not fire at him and as far as I could see nor did anyone else, he went straight into the sea. I was so astonished I could not believe my eyes.

'While I was watching for others there was a crash behind my head. A bullet came through my hood, passed through the back of my helmet, tore through the back of my goggles, and before I knew where I was the hood had flown back and my goggles had disappeared. After that all I could see were enemy bombers and fighters going like mad for home.'

No other Fighter Command pilot seems to have experienced anything quite so strange as the Messerschmitt's apparent suicide dive, but all were able to meet the German advance blow for blow. And before lunch-time it was clear that the first rake of the Eagle's claws had been less than successful.

Yet with no sign of the weather breaking, the forces of Kesselring and Sperrle returned again in the afternoon. Fifty bombers from Luftflotte 2 with a strong

# Into the Jaws...!

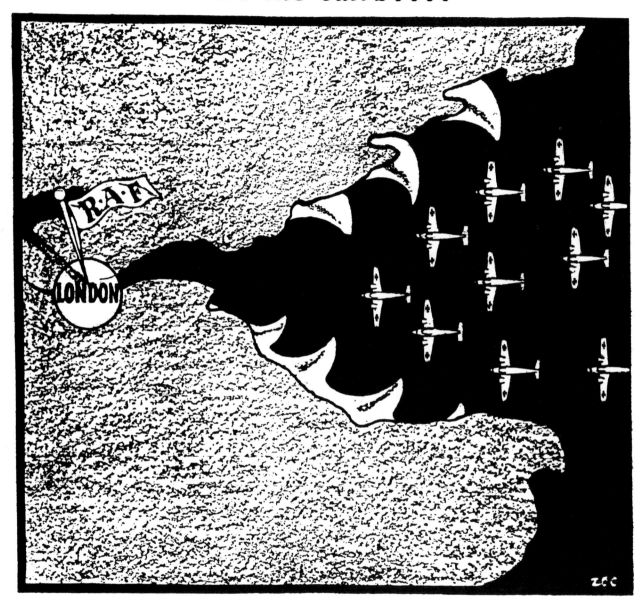

*'Eagle Day' as seen by the* Daily Mirror*'s political cartoonist 'Zec'.*

fighter escort headed up the Thames Estuary once more, while forty more accompanied by fighters struck at the Southampton dockside and air bases around Salisbury Plain. Again with a full half-hour warning of their approach, Fighter Command had its men and machines in position in good time.

Another anonymous flight lieutenant provided newspapers with this account of the second meeting of the attackers and defenders in the sky above the south coast on Eagle Day.

'The air was filled with Nazi aircraft. There seemed to be thousands of Messerschmitts, Spitfires and Hurri-

canes all mixed up in a series of dog fights. The three Hurricanes I was leading concentrated on a group of six Messerschmitts. I saw one of the others shoot down his Messerschmitt and the other pilot of the flight fire a long burst at another Messerschmitt. He broke away when only twenty-five yards from the German machine, which went streaming down towards the sea – but we did not see it crash into the water, so we have not claimed it as a victim.

'Oil poured from another Messerschmitt which I had attacked, covering not only my windscreen but my entire aircraft. I followed him down and saw him crash

*An early German victim on Eagle Day, shot down on the Essex coast near Clacton. (overleaf) Not all Fighter Command pilots escaped unscathed on Eagle Day – this RAF pilot, who had to bale out, was rescued from the Channel by an alert air–sea rescue launch.*

into the water. I climbed back to 15,000 feet and saw a Messerschmitt chasing a Hurricane. I dived on its tail to sea level. He zoomed up to 5000 feet. I followed, and after my first burst of fire he blew up in the air, and I watched pieces of flaming aircraft fall into the sea.'

The incredible resistance and resilience with which Fighter Command responded on that Tuesday was not only more than its leaders might have dared hope for, but was certainly beyond anything that Kesselring and Sperrle had anticipated. In all, the Germans flew 1000 fighter sorties and nearly 500 bomber raids. The RAF countered with 700 sorties – but to far greater effect, as Basil Collier has also commented. 'The big punch on which Goering counted to lure British fighter squadrons to their doom had cost him 45 aircraft lost against 13 aircraft (but only seven pilots) lost by Dowding. Beginning with high hopes, the Germans had taken the first step to failure.'

As evening fell on 13 August, there was an almost palpable feeling among the people of England that something very significant had occurred – a feeling underlined by the evidence that lay before their eyes across the countryside of more wrecked and burning

aircraft than had ever been seen before on any single day. This impression was also reflected in the national newspapers the following morning – a morning which dawned with even poorer visibility, enabling the population to savour the news over their breakfast tables while across the Channel the German Luftflotten fretted, unable to take to the skies to renew their attack.

Under larger-than-usual headlines such as 'All Day Air Battles in Channel', readers were informed of the heavy losses that the raiders had suffered – although to be fair the figures quoted were somewhat inflated. Side by side with these stories ran accounts of the 'absurd' claims German radio stations had been making the previous evening that 'The Luftwaffe has won control over Dover!' Several British newspapers also quoted the CBS Radio news broadcaster Ed Murrow, who in a

(right) *Triumphant front page of the* Daily Express *of Tuesday 13 August.*

**BEAR BRAND** PURE SILK STOCKINGS

# Daily Express

No. 12,550    Tuesday, August 13, 1940    One Penny

**GET FIT** BOURN-VITA 9d. PER QTR. LB.

## The Battle of Britain is on: Hitler throws in more and more bombers

# BIGGEST AIR RAIDS OF ALL

## *R.A.F. shoots down 39 more Nazis and loses only nine fighters*

### PORTSMOUTH HEAVILY BOMBED

*Daily Express Air Reporter BASIL CARDEW*

**H**ITLER intensified his mass air raids on British ports still further yesterday. Even more aircraft than he used in the mass attacks on Thursday and Sunday were sent against Portsmouth and the Kent coast.

**Afterthoughts on raiding Britain by**

## FIVE CAPTURED RAIDERS

*Here are stories sent from five south-east coast towns last night :—*

**THE REALIST**

A BADLY wounded German airman came down by parachute in a field. A farm groom covered him with a shotgun. The airman flung up his hands.

And then he said : "No more fighting. English too good."

**THE PHILOSOPHER**

CRIPPLED by a British fighter, a Messerschmitt made a forced landing in a field of cabbages. The thirty-year-old pilot, an officer wearing several decorations, stepped out with his hands above his head, gave himself up to a farm hand.

And then he said : "These Spitfires are very good. They were too fast for me. So I'm out of it now."

**THE FINANCIER**

RIDDLED with Hurricane bullets and shrapnel, a Heinkel bomber crashed in a field. All five of the crew parachuted and were captured. The pilot was the last to be found.

And then he said : "A shell got the port engine. A shell cut the middle engine. A million marks gone !"

**THE GROUSER**

ANOTHER Messerschmitt made a forced landing among corn stooks at Berwick, eight miles from Eastbourne. He was wounded in the shoulder. He was taken prisoner by an Army sergeant.

And then he said : "That's what we get for coming to England."

**AND THE ITALIAN**

A JUNKERS 88 was shot down over Portland. One of the four airmen, who all parachuted to safety, was an Italian. He fell in the sea and was rescued.

And then he said : "Yes, I am an Italian. I was fighting for the Germans."

All day long there were terrific battles over the Channel and along the coast. And last night the Air Ministry announced we had shot down thirty-nine more Germans and had lost nine R.A.F. fighters. The German official news agency claim seventy-one British planes down, and admit nineteen Germans missing.

After dark last night the raiders returned—over the south-east, the south-west, north-east, and Wales. At midnight it was reported that bombs had been dropped in one south-east area.

Although fewer German aircraft were shot down yesterday the ratio in favour of the R.A.F. is almost doubled. On Thursday it was nearly three and a half to one; on Sunday it dropped to two and a half to one; and yesterday it was nearly four and a half to one.

Here is the battle-record since the mass raids began :—

| | German losses. | British losses. |
|---|---|---|
| Thursday | 61 | 18 |
| Friday | 1 | 0 |
| Saturday | 1 | 1 |
| Sunday | 61 | 26 |
| Monday | 39 | 9 |
| Total | 163 | 54 |

He gave his life to save town . .

" **A**N R.A.F. plane, flames spreading from airscrew to tail, came crashing towards the centre of a south-east town. The pilot stuck to his controls, skimmed rooftops—by feet, it seemed—and sacrificed his life by crashing into the sea."

You remember the story. Here is the hero—Flying Officer D. N. Grice, of Park-hill, Ealing. He was twenty-eight; was married nine months ago to Miss Margaret Peal, of Ealing.

The mayor of the town he saved has received subscriptions from many citizens who wish the heroism of Flying Officer Grice to be commemorated.

### DOCTOR OPERATED AS BOMBS BURST

*Daily Express Staff Reporter BERNARD HALL*
PORTSMOUTH, Monday.

**T**WENTY-FIVE bombers, remnants of a much larger force broken up and dispersed over the Channel by the R.A.F., carried out the twenty-minute raid on Portsmouth at noon today.

#### 3 lbs. 13 ozs. of shell

*Misses a gardener*

While a gardener in a south-east coastal town was weeding yesterday, a piece of shell whistled over his bent back and buried itself beside him.

The shell fragment was 7ins. long, 8ins. wide and 1¼ins. thick, and weighed 3lbs. 13ozs.

#### Crown Princess will be Roosevelt's guest

STOCKHOLM, Monday.—The Norwegian legation in Stockholm announced today that Crown Princess Martha and her children—Ragnhild (aged ten), Astrid (seven), and Harald (three)—have left Stockholm for the United States, where they will be the guests of President Roosevelt.—A.P.

━ **BACK PAGE, COLUMN FOUR**

I watched part of the raid from the centre of the city. Anti-aircraft fire from shore batteries and warships was terrific. Hardly had the first raider arrived when the sky for miles was a closely woven pattern of white and black shell-bursts—thousands of them.

French naval ratings shot off the tail of one machine. It crashed, and a German parachuted from it into the middle of a street. Four other Nazis were captured—two on mudflats in the harbour. Six German bombers were shot down.

#### ON DENSE AREA

Twenty-one bombs fell in the most densely populated areas of the city; some of the bombers machine-gunned the ground as they passed. A railway station was partly destroyed. Among the casualties was a four-month-old baby, one of three members of a family who were killed. But the record of escapes is astonishing.

An elderly surgeon, a specialist famous in the south, was carrying out a critical mastoid operation on a woman patient. A bomb burst in a narrow street a few yards outside the hospital. With his staff of five the surgeon carried on, and completed the operation.

The nurses' wing of the hospital caught fire. But it was empty. The nightduty nurses who had been sleeping there were all out. In the flooded corridor outside one room I found a book. It was entitled "With Four Walls : a classic of escape."

#### HOSES IN POND

The bomb burst a water main, and the crater filled with a constantly renewed supply of water. Firemen used the "pond " for their hoses to put but the blaze.

At this very point Lord Nelson left his hotel on that famous morning in 1805 to go to Trafalgar. The path he took down the street to Sally Port was splintered today with wreckage and splinters.

Nearby, an old parish hall used as a rest-room by A.R.P. staff was hit and set on fire. But the staff had just left it to go on duty. They returned to salvage their property.

A church was hit. But the vicar was at a cemetery conducting a funeral. His wife and child took refuge in the basement of the vicarage and escaped injury.

A big bomb fell in the middle of a road near a park. But it missed buildings on both sides. Windows were splintered.

One other oddity of the raid : the Guildhall clock has a twisted hand. It was hit by a bomb fragment.

And that is all. Net result : damage to war effort, slight; morale of the population, stronger than ever.

Tip for next time : Keep under cover.

#### Aliens' camps visited

SIMLA, Monday.—Captain H. L. V. Russell and one Indian soldier were killed in a recent engagement with hostile tribes on the Banno-N'zan Shah road (North-West Frontier). It was announced in Simla today. Fourteen Indians were wounded, and one is missing.—Reuter.

### 'Britain's new terrifying weapon'

NEW YORK, Monday.

**A**MERICAN newspapers, finding their most exciting news today in Britain's defeat of German air attacks; prominently display stories of a "new and terrifying British weapon."

They say Britain has a gun which fires steel cables to snare German planes, and that the new one-inch pom-pom gun may supply an answer to the dive bomber.

Berlin claims of staggering victories in today's air battles are generally discounted in the New York evening papers, whose headlines emphasise the Nazi losses while the German figures for British planes shot down are printed in small type.

#### BALLOON TRY-OUT

Sailors who man the ships that guard and feed industrial Britain believe that the aide which finds the answer to the dive-bomber has won the war—and they think Britain has found or is finding it, writes an A.P. war correspondent.

The answer would be an anti-aircraft gun plus the balloon barrage, which convoys appear to be trying out. The balloons keep the bombers high enough to prevent accurate bombing and if they come low the new guns get them.

The gun is a many-barrelled pompom which lets off a bundle of inch or more shells, constructed so delicately that they explode on the slightest contact.

#### U.S. mission 'a step towards war'

*Says American admiral*

*Daily Express Staff Reporter*
NEW YORK, Monday.—One of the most significant steps taken by President Roosevelt, according to Admiral Yates Sterling, U.S. Navy (retired), is the despatch to London of the special naval mission headed by Rear-Admiral Robert Ghormley.

Admiral Sterling said that at present mission may be for the purpose of finding out just how seriously Britain needs our active help to obtain victory or to see how if the possibility of a British defeat seems imminent.

"An increasing section of American naval opinion in my observation tends to the belief that we cannot afford to have Britain defeated and her fleet made derelict.

"This trend is towards American participation in the war if the possibility of a British defeat seems imminent. Admiral Ghormley's mission may be the preliminary step towards that eventuality."

#### Even conversation rationed in Paris

*Daily Express Correspondent*

GENEVA, Monday.—Goods are not the only things restricted in France. Conversation between shopkeeper and customer has also been reduced, says the Petit Parisien, which gives the following list of expressions in the daily life of France since the German invasion :—

Shopkeeper : I've sold out.
Car owner : Not a single drop. And how about you ?
Housewife : Have you any butter ?
Baker : Give me your ration coupon.
Grocer : No sugar.
Coal merchant : I am expecting fresh supplies soon.

#### Russia expecting bumper harvest

Pravda, official newspaper of Russia's Communist Party, reported yesterday that the Soviet harvest this year is likely to be much better than that of most recent years.

Crops are extremely good, the newspaper said, but difficulty was being experienced in getting farmers to deliver their quota of grain to the State.

#### Nazis jail rumour-monger for life

BERLIN, Monday.— An Austrian, Eduard Grabher, has been sentenced to the maximum penalty, penal servitude for life, by the Nazi People's Court for spreading rumours in Switzerland that Germany intended to invade that country, says the German News Agency tonight.

After the Austrian anschluss, Grabher fled to Switzerland, where he told an officer of the Swiss Army that German troops and military detachments were ready to invade Switzerland. Later he was expelled from Switzerland.—Reuter.

#### Finns found league to fight for liberty

A League of "Veterans" of last year's Russo-Finnish war has been founded "to strengthen the unanimous will of the Finnish people to defend their independence in any circumstances," said Helsinki radio last night.

#### British officer killed

NEW YORK, Monday.—Patric Knowles and Conn Tapley, young British film actors, in Hollywood left for Ottawa today to offer themselves to the Royal Canadian Air Force.

### ALBANIANS KILL 400 ITALIANS

*Belgrade report*

BELGRADE, Monday.

**A**N unconfirmed report from the Albanian frontier received in Belgrade states that 10,000 Albanians are in revolt, and that 400 Italian soldiers have been killed in Albania.

Three Italian warships with troops aboard are said to have arrived at Durazzo, the Albanian port, yesterday.

M. Musa Juka, former Albanian Minister of the Interior, is reported to be among the rebels.—B.U.P.

Italian plots exposed.—Page Two.

### Former A.R.P. chief held

*Daily Express Staff Reporter*

BOURNEMOUTH, Monday.
MR. H. G. D. BARRETT, who was appointed as area A.R.P. staff officer for Bournemouth, Christchurch and Poole in October 1938, and who resigned early last June, has been arrested by the Bournemouth police.

When he resigned no statement was made. Before coming to Bournemouth Mr. Barrett was A.R.P. organiser for St. Pancras, N.W. He had previously travelled extensively in France, Spain and Germany, where he is understood to have studied air raid precautions. He holds a B.Sc. degree.

---

## STOP PRESS

#### MOUNTAIN GRAVE FOR SIR ABE BAILEY

CAPETOWN, Monday.—Sir Abe Bailey will be buried at Muizenberg on Thursday afternoon on the mountainside above his house.—Reuter.

#### FRICK TO INSPECT OCCUPIED FRANCE

Dr. Frick, German Minister of the Interior, has arrived in Strasbourg on a tour of inspection of the occupied western territories.—Reuter.

#### B.B.C. FADES OUT

B.B.C. Home Service programme was faded out on certain wavelengths just before eleven o'clock in interests of national security. It was still possible to get clear reception on an alternative wavelength.

#### Mr. Coward has plans for "after the war"

#### Three little girls buried alive

*They were filling sandbags*

Three little girls helping to fill sandbags in Fordham, Cambs, yesterday, were buried alive when a wall of the pit gave way. Three other children partly buried were rescued.

---

## And WE did this to THEM

THE crew of an R.A.F. aircraft which bombed a synthetic oil plant at Dortmund, in the Ruhr, during Sunday night, reported that they saw and HEARD an explosion of exceptional violence.

The attack took place in darkness and cloud, but soon after midnight an early raider saw four of its bombs fall on the oil plant, to be followed by a big blue flash.

An hour later another aircraft took up the attack. After a salvo of its heavy bombs had struck the plant, there was a violent explosion, and even though they were flying at several thousand feet the crew could hear it above the roar of their engines.

In most cases the engines drown the noise of the explosions.

That was the high spot of a series of raids which cost us three planes.

Oil was again the main objective. The plants at Gelsenkirchen and Wanne-Eickel were heavily bombed. Other aircraft attacked the depot at Cherbourg.

A successful bombing from high altitudes was a feature of daylight raids by medium bombers when, for the third day running, Le Bourg airfield at Guernsey was bombed.

*[Map caption:]* ENGLAND · LONDON · GERMAN CLAIMS IN WHITE PANELS. BRITISH STATEMENTS IN BLACK PANELS.

---

"WELL, DID YOU BEARD THE LION IN HIS DEN?"
"NO, HE MET ME OUTSIDE."

Daily Express, *13 August 1940.*

*A burning Heinkel HE 111 being chased back across the English Channel by a Spitfire.*

despatch from London said that during the day he had been privileged to watch 'the toughest fighters on earth in action', and added, 'If one must be bombed, one could not ask for better company.'

Murrow, in fact, was to play a significant part in keeping alive the faith of ordinary Americans in Britain while their Government remained firmly neutral towards the war. He also publicised the fact that a number of young Americans had crossed the Atlantic to join in the battle as fighter pilots in the RAF. (It was not, incidentally, until later in the year that the now-famous Eagle Squadron composed entirely of US pilots was formed.)

Among those who fought on Eagle Day was Pilot Officer Jim Daley of Amarillo in Texas whom Murrow

persuaded to broadcast to the USA. And as his voice carried across the Atlantic with its mixture of boyish enthusiasm and courage, it certainly deeply affected many of those who heard it.

'I have never been so tickled in my life when we were sent to the Channel to look for trouble today,' Daley said. 'It was the Germans who found it. At 10,000 feet we saw five Messerschmitt 109s, and somewhere around us was a large party of bombers. We sailed into them right away and our squadron leader set the example immediately by cracking down on a Messerschmitt. He and another pilot saw it crash into the sea.

'Then another pilot chased an enemy aircraft towards France and shot bits off the machine. I had a good crack at one, but suddenly two other Messerschmitts attacked me. Something hit the fuselage, shaking the machine a bit, but we quickly recovered. When I was whirling around the sky another Messerschmitt fired into my windscreen. I had another crack at him before he disappeared. Then we came home. I wouldn't have missed this for all the Japs in China!'

It was thanks to the courage of Jim Daley and all his British colleagues that the German airmen were now well aware that they were, indeed, facing a bunch of 'tough fighters' – a fact that was confirmed by Luftwaffe pilots such as the pair who were shot down over England and quoted in a report in the *Daily Mail* of 14 August.

'"Those Spitfires are very good. This is my heaven – I am out of it," said a German pilot in a good accent while his wounds were being attended to after his aeroplane had been forced down near a south-east coast town yesterday. The pilot had walked towards a farm worker with his hands up and said, "A cigarette and a cup of tea please." Another German pilot said in broken English, "Shell cut the port engine, shell cut the middle engine. Million marks gone now."'

The pages of the press also contained more down-to-earth tales of the impact of *Adler Tag* on ordinary men and women. The *Daily Express*, for instance, ran a special column of 'things heroic, and tragic, and purely comic, jostling one another in a twelve-hour fantasy of life and death'. These items are typical of how the men and women on the ground reacted to the crucial events happening above them in the skies.

And as those same people again looked up at the lowering grey clouds and wondered how long it would be before the Germans returned – as they surely would – they had no way of knowing that there was worse to come. Much worse. But, equally, a triumph that was ultimately to echo down the halls of history for ever.

*Pilots of Fighter Command report back to base on their successes during Eagle Day.*

American film star Douglas Fairbanks Jnr, in his uniform as an officer of the US Navy Reserve. He broadcast to Britain in August 1940.

# THE FRIENDSHIP BRIDGE
## US Film Star Douglas Fairbanks Jnr Broadcasts From New York

I have been anxious to make a broadcast to Britain for some time. Now that I have the opportunity I find it difficult to put into words the things that I should like to say, because Britain to me is more than a second home; it is *another* home. I count as some of the happiest hours of my life those that I have spent in various places from John o' Groats to Land's End.

Since the war, many of us on this side of the water have tried to convince our people not only that you are our nearest relations, with whom we have every kind of emotional and cultural bond, but that for our own future safety and security the best move we could make would be to extend every kind of aid we could within our, then, limited means. It was very difficult at first, particularly in California where I work. The Atlantic is three thousand miles away, and the intervening miles had a tendency to make people feel that they were not in any danger. That feeling has almost disappeared now. The people out West are now aware that nobody is safe, in this war, and when the *Blitzkrieg* really got going they realised for the first time in what danger they were. You cannot imagine what effect the miracles you have been achieving in throwing back this *Blitzkrieg* have had there.

I remember when I was on the set in a studio in Hollywood making a film, all work was suspended while we listened to Mr Churchill; the carpenters and electricians, the technical men, as well as members of the cast, were as emotionally moved and thrilled as any of you who heard it in Britain; in fact, they cheered at the end. Again, when His Majesty the King spoke, I cannot exaggerate our emotion as we listened to his words. One tough old carpenter, who is almost a double of Victor McLaglen, said to me: 'Doug, I don't think much of Europeans, they're a crazy lot at best, but these British guys are *our* people: they belong to the same family. We must do everything we can to help them, and anybody who thinks otherwise ought to be ashamed of themselves.'

Now, those words were typical of the spirit which is sweeping over this country today. You have probably heard a lot about our Isolationists, but they are disappearing faster than the buffaloes and Red Indians of eighty years ago. The other day I was asked to speak to about twenty-five thousand people in Chicago. It was a plea for more and quicker aid of every kind for Britain. This section of the country was supposed to be the centre of Isolationism; it is where Lindbergh and his group generally hold forth. Well, the enthusiasm showed pretty clearly that the Isolationists are in full retreat.

I have just returned from my small farm in the South – Virginia. The people there are nearly all of British descent. One of the farmers said to me the other day that he is trying to double his output next year. When I asked him why, he appeared shocked that I should not know the answer. He said: 'I must dig just like they're doing on the other side. I hope most of it is going over there,' and he waved his hand in the general direction of the Atlantic Ocean, as though Britain were the next county.

About the Southern States it may interest you to know that the majority of the United States Volunteers to the British Army come from there. They are going up to Canada in droves, and I hear that they insist, in their slow Southern drawl, that they come from British Columbia.

You may be interested to know also that the movies are trying to do their bit, too, and most storymakers are attempting to inject as much pro-British feeling into their pictures as the theoretically neutral censors will allow. We have been helped by the British Colony in Hollywood. Many of them served with distinction the last time you chaps stood in the breach. Those British members of our community out there have been grand ambassadors on this side, and through their contacts with the public have been perhaps partly responsible for the reawakening which is now sweeping America.

When I was in Washington recently, I was in touch with some of the biggest men in our Government services. Naturally, as officials, they are not as easily swayed by the emotional aspect of the situation as they are by the cold, hard facts of national self-interest. Yet all of them told me that for our own self-preservation there was no alternative but to bend every effort to send Britain all the help we could. They realise the immensity of the task. They also realise how long it will take us to build up our own defences. The people know it, too, as they showed in their acceptance of conscription, which, for the first time in both of our histories, has been introduced in peace time. Now, doesn't that make you feel happier about our youth which sometimes gets damaging publicity?

I feel very humble in talking to you at all, because many of us Americans are now realising that you are fighting for us as well as for yourselves and we feel that talking is a poor way of expressing our gratitude. As you know, our national resources are at your disposal, but what we should like most to say, and that with the most profound sincerity, is 'Thank you, and God bless you.'

Radio broadcast
August 1940

# Bathroom used as prison to hold German airman

## COUNCIL MEETS IN REFUGE

*Daily Express Staff Reporter*

*HERE are some of the things that happened during yesterday's raids; things heroic, and tragic, and purely comic, jostling one another in a twelve-hour fantasy of life and death.*

### In the drink

A Dornier, riddled with a Spitfire's bullets, fled south over the Thames estuary. Suddenly its tail snapped off and the bomber crashed – in a field near some houses.

When householders hurried over they found two of the crew badly injured, the other two unhurt.

They took the uninjured men to a house and decided that they had better be separated.

So one of the Germans was invited to take a bath. He accepted – and was locked in the bathroom until soldiers arrived.

*Daily Express*
14 August 1940

### Bullet? No, tea

Mrs Betty Tylee and Miss Jean Smithson were first to reach the young pilot of a Messerschmitt when it was shot down by an RAF fighter.

He was lying some distance from his machine and he wore the Iron Cross. His first question, in very good English: 'Are you going to shoot me now?'

'No,' said Mrs Tylee 'We don't do that in England. Would you like a cup of tea?'

'Yes, please,' he said eagerly.

So they made the Nazi airman a cup of tea. Then the ambulance called to take him to hospital.

### Moved, seconded

A meeting of the rural council was being held in a south-eastern district when raiders were reported in the area.

Solemnly the chairman rose and proposed: 'That this meeting do adjourn to an air-raid shelter.'

Solemnly a councillor rose: 'I beg to second the motion.'

Solemnly the councillors raised their hands. The chairman declared the motion carried. And solemnly they walked to an air-raid shelter where the business of the meeting was continued.

### Cat stays on

Mr and Mrs Alfred Smith were walking through the streets of a south-eastern town yesterday when a raid began. They carried a jug and a saucer, and they were going to their old home, destroyed by bombs a month ago.

They went on walking during the raid because they were expected – by Smuts, their cat.

Although Mr and Mrs Smith have a new home, Smuts refuses to leave the bricks and wood where he always lived. They have tried everything to get him away. Now they are resigned to taking the cat his food every day among the ruins of their own home.

### As one was buried . . .

Overhead on the south-east coast raged a terrific air battle. Below, a funeral procession wound its slow way to the cemetery.

Men in RAF uniform carried the coffin. An RAF chaplain conducted the service.

Above, one of the Nazi planes fell in black smoke.

Below, the mourners lowered into its grave the body of a young German airman, brought down four days earlier.

### Boy saves baby

When bombs fell in another south-east town a fifteen-year-old boy flung himself over his baby brother as glass splintered over them. The boy was slightly cut; the baby was unhurt.

### Farmer's greeting

A Messerschmitt crashed in a cornfield in which the farmer was reaping. The farmer dismounted and went over to the Nazi pilot. 'Hi!' he said. 'What do you mean by it? You nearly crashed atop of me and my reaper.'

*Front page of the Illustrated London News commemorating the Fighter Command success on Eagle Day.*

# —7—

# BLOODY THURSDAY – AND THE GREAT PARACHUTE RUSE

It was not only the debris of crashed German aircraft that confronted people living across the southern half of England on the morning of Wednesday 14 August. For also scattered over the countryside were a large number of . . . *empty parachutes*. As another dismal, cloudy morning broke over the nation, surprised men and women discovered the parachutes spreadeagled over rooftops, hanging limply from trees or lying abandoned in fields. There could be no mistaking what they were – but *where* were the parachutists?

Those fearing the worst wondered if there had been a German invasion during the night. But if there had been, why had nothing been said on the BBC News? For it was now the habit of virtually everyone in the kingdom to turn on their wireless sets as soon as they woke up to hear any news there might be about the battle for Britain – and certainly on this morning there had been no mention of an enemy landing.

Those who found the abandoned parachutes undoubtedly had an anxious wait until the mystery was solved. However, those who came across the large pieces of billowing silk hanging from the branches of trees with their harnesses still clasped together had more reason to be puzzled than alarmed. While the rest, who discovered parachutes on the ground still packed inside their containers, wondered whether it might all be a giant hoax.

Indeed, it took a little while for the whole story to emerge that dank August morning. In some districts, it appeared, the parachutes had actually been seen falling from the darkened skies, and when Home Guards had rushed to the spot they were more than a little surprised to find them empty. The sound of the metal containers falling on to rooftops had also awakened a number of people, and their immediate reactions had been to call the police, though they, too, were puzzled at not seeing or hearing anyone in the vicinity.

To further heighten the mystery, when some of the packages were examined they were found to contain documents and maps which gave all the appearance of being instructions for a major German operation. So *where* were the troops to carry it out?

As the reports were coordinated, however, it became evident that there had not been a single German attached to any of the parachutes. And when one of the containers was found 'in a place and in circumstances which made it obvious that the Germans intended it to fall into the hands of the military authorities' (to quote an official statement issued by the Ministry of Information the following day), the cat was clearly out of the bag.

It had all been a German ruse to spread panic. Based on the reports the Ministry had received from across the country, it was now in a position to call the events of Tuesday night 'a clumsy effort to cause alarm, which it has notably failed to do'. As well as exposing the purpose of the empty parachutes, the Ministry statement added: 'The documents in the bags have been examined and are clearly not genuine instructions. It is evident the whole incident was organised by the Germans as an aid to their defeatist propaganda which they have for a long time been attempting to carry on in this country by wireless

*Cartoonist Nicolas Bentley's famous comment on the German parachutist invasion scare.*

" *Eh ?* "

*One of the hundreds of empty German parachutes dropped on England on 17 August as a ruse to make the population believe an aerial invasion had taken place. (right) Examining some of the maps and instructions found with the parachutes.*

and other means. If any further evidence of this was needed, it is to be found in a false account of the affair from the German broadcasting station masquerading as British which was evidently prepared *before* the incident even took place!'

The story of this ruse that failed brought a little light relief to the people of Britain that Wednesday morning – while the inclement weather also brought them respite from any Luftwaffe operations. Undoubtedly, though, Goering's pilots across the Channel were anxious to get back into action after the bloody nose they had been given on Tuesday.

When the Reichsmarschall ordered his men into the air on 15 August for their second day of major operations, it was to be the first – and only – time when all his operational aircraft were utilised. In all, the Luftwaffe flew 1786 sorties, the most flown on any single day of the entire battle. Fighter Command, in reply, flew 974. Not without some justification, I think, it has been suggested by some historians that the British achievements on this day were such that it perhaps ought to be the date on which the Battle of Britain is annually commemorated, rather than the accepted date a month later.

In any event, it was on this clear August day that Goering's Luftflotte 5, under the command of General Stumpff, also joined the fray, attacking across the North

Sea from their bases in Norway and Denmark, while Kesselring and Sperrle marauded up from the south once again. It was, though, a plan that depended for its success on Dowding's forces having already been severely weakened – which, of course, they had not been – and the resultant battle was to go down in newspaper headlines as 'Bloody Thursday'.

Despite the fact that the weight of the German attacks on Tuesday had come from across the Channel, Dowding had not allowed himself to be panicked into moving back-up aircraft from his bases in the Midlands and north down to the south-east. In fact, such a move would have been quite contrary to his nature, and the disposition of his forces remained virtually unchanged throughout the entire battle, though he did 'rest' hard-pressed squadrons by rotating them between 'active' and 'quiet' sectors. And so the chief and his men were fully prepared when, shortly after noon on 15 August, following a morning of only sporadic attacks from France, radar reported a large contingent of enemy aircraft about 100 miles from the Firth of Forth.

Stumpff's directive was to attack aerodromes in Northumberland and Yorkshire, and his force consisted of approximately 85 Heinkel 111s, 50 Junkers 88s and 45 Messerschmitt 110s, the fighters being fitted with special supplementary fuel tanks so that they could make the long journey protecting the bombers. Opposing him was Air Vice-Marshal Saul who had in immediate operation three squadrons of Spitfires, one of Hurricanes and one of Blenheims – with three and a half stand-by squadrons to call to his assistance if required. Although he had no way of knowing it at the time, Saul was about to confront and drive off the one and only major German daylight offensive launched from Scandinavia against the north.

With their early warning of the German forces' imminent arrival, Saul's Spitfires – though outnumbered – were able to gain a height advantage over their attackers and tear into them with devastating effect. When the Hurricanes and Blenheims were also called into action, the men of Luftflotte 5 found themselves being decisively driven back before they could have any major stategic impact, though some bomb damage was caused to both military and civilian properties. The British tactics proved a triumph of organisation, and in the final analysis cost Stumpff one-sixth of his entire Luftflotte.

Things had not gone so well for Fighter Command in the south, however, where a force of 40 of Kesselring's dive bombers had inflicted considerable damage on Air Vice-Marshal Keith Park's sector, while Sperrle's men had bombed aerodromes in Kent, Sussex and Surrey causing the loss of valuable planes and equipment.

But still, by the end of the day the Eagle's second strike had brought Goering no nearer to success than

VIEWED FROM THE GROUND, INVADING GLIDERS WOULD BE DISTINGUISHABLE BY THE WIDE SPAN OF THE WINGS, COMPARED WITH THE LENGTH OF THE BODY; AND OF COURSE THEIR FLIGHT IS SILENT. THE WIDE SPAN OF A TROOP-CARRYING GLIDER IS VERY EVIDENT WHEN COMPARED WITH THAT OF A TROOP-CARRYING, POWER-DRIVEN AIRCRAFT.

GERMAN 'JU 52' TROOP-CARRYING AEROPLANE.

TROOP-CARRYING GLIDERS.

the first. What he had hoped would be decisive strikes had been effectively repulsed, and the cost in destroyed aircraft was such that the Luftwaffe was never again to fly so many sorties in a single day. The final total was 75 losses to the Germans and 34 to Fighter Command, a fact which caused *The Times* next day to break with tradition and run a jubilant front-page headline alongside its title: 'Nazi Air Losses Still Soaring'. Both the *Daily Express* and the *News Chronicle* hailed the event quite simply as 'Victory on Bloody Thursday!' while the *Daily Telegraph*, in its stalwart fashion, reassured its readers that there was no truth in a dastardly story put out by German propagandists that the British flag flying on Nelson's famous ship HMS *Victory*, berthed in Portsmouth Harbour, had been struck down during the bombing! Explaining what the German radio had attempted to magnify into an incident not far removed from the fall of the British Empire, the *Telegraph* stated: 'There is no truth in the claim that German aircraft struck down the Admiral's flag from HMS *Victory* and it fell into the water. As the flagship of the port, the *Victory* carries the flag of Admiral Sir William James, Commander-in-Chief. This flag flew uninjured throughout the raid and is still flying as everyone in the town can see – besides which, *Victory* lies in the dry dock and there is no water nearby!'

Thanks to the energy of Beaverbrook and his work force, Dowding was able immediately to replace his lost aircraft and be ready for another German onslaught which, as the weather remained good, followed the next day. That the German pilots attacked once more in such good heart was doubtless due to the reports from their commanders (incorrect, as it transpired) that the RAF had lost almost 600 aircraft since the beginning of July and was surely on its last legs. Fighter Command, the Luftwaffe leaders said, probably had no more than 300 serviceable planes it could muster that day. In actual fact, the true figures reveal the British losses to have been half that estimate, and their strength almost double it. That said, it was still true that German fighter aircraft outnumbered Dowding's machines two to one.

August 16 proved one of the few successful days for the Luftwaffe in the skies over Britain, skies that were treacherously bright and clear for the first time in over a week. On this third day of major operations, the Germans flew only marginally fewer sorties than the previous day – 1715 – and caused considerable damage to several important aerodromes. In the air they lost a total of 45 aircraft to Fighter Command's 21, though as many as 60 RAF machines were destroyed where they were lined up on the ground.

The most devastating German attacks were made

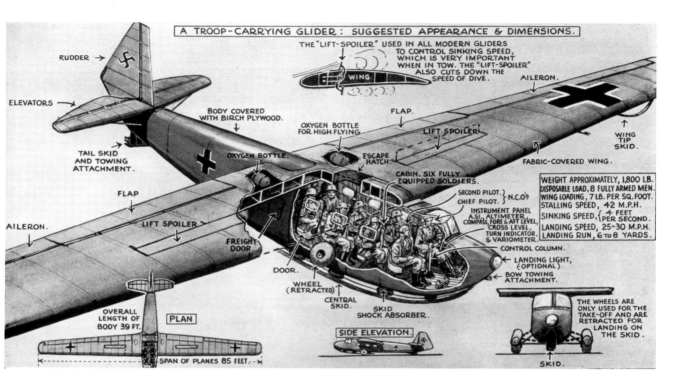

on the base at Tangmere – where 14 aircraft were destroyed or seriously damaged, the worst such single blow suffered by Fighter Command – and at a naval airport at Gosport. It was during the attack on Gosport that a proud moment in RAF history occurred when Flight Lieutenant J.B. Nicolson, a twenty-three-year-old pilot belonging to No. 249 Squadron from the Middle Wallop sector, kept on fighting despite being badly injured and with his aircraft on fire, to win the first Victoria Cross awarded to a Fighter Command pilot. Later, Flt Lieut. Nicolson recounted his extraordinary day which had seen both bravery and a touch of comedy (for after baling out of his Hurricane he was shot at by Home Guard officers who mistook him for a German!) in a memorable BBC radio broadcast which is reprinted on page 122. This understated personal memoir, in which he made no mention of the mix-up with the Home Guard nor that he was under intensive care for forty-eight hours after his ordeal, served as an enormous boost to the nation's morale. (See 'What a Fool!')

As a matter of record, two days after Nicolson won his VC, three WAAFs won Military Medals for their bravery during a German raid on the Fighter Command station at Biggin Hill. For exceptional courage and coolness during the raid when they were in very real danger from unexploded bombs, the medals

*'Watch for Nazi Gliders!' Two of a series of illustrations published in the summer of 1940 to inform the British public of the dangers they should be on the look-out for.*

*(overleaf) 'A Panorama of Disaster' – two pages of photographs from the* Illustrated London News *graphically showing Fighter Command's achievements in the middle of August 1940.*

# A PANORAMA OF NAZI DISASTER: SOME OF THE 493

TWO CRASHED GERMAN 'PLANES ON A SOUTH-EAST COAST BEACH.

A WRECK NEAR HOOE, ON THE HASTINGS ROAD.

RETRIBUTION ON ONE OF EASTBOURNE'S COWARDLY ATTACKERS.

AN "INQUEST" IN PROGRESS ON THE REMAINS OF A RAIDER.

THE REMAINS OF A MESSERSCHMITT "110" BURIED DEEP IN THE GROUND.

KEEPING GUARD BY THE WRECKAGE OF A JUNKERS "88."

A MESSERSCHMITT'S END "AMID THE ALIEN CORN."

ACCEPTABLE SCRAP-METAL IS ALL THAT REMAINS OF THIS 'PLANE.

The astonishing total of 493 German aeroplanes shot down in one week only includes those definitely known to be destroyed. Whatever the rate of German aircraft production, it cannot keep pace with this devastation, while pilots and air crews cannot conceivably be trained at such a rate. Tribute must be paid

PHOTOGRAPHS BY KEYSTONE, A.P., G.P.U., WIDE

# GERMAN AEROPLANES BROUGHT DOWN IN ONE WEEK.

A JUNKERS "88" SHOT DOWN ON AUGUST 12.

A.F.S. MEN SPRAYING THE REMAINS OF A NAZI FIGHTER.

A FALLEN ENEMY 'PLANE—BURNT COMPLETELY OUT.

A BULLET-RIDDLED GERMAN BOMBER DOWN NEAR THE SOUTH COAST.

A MACHINE WHICH STRUCK A MOUNTAIN PEAK IN SCOTLAND.

THE WRECK OF ONE OF AUGUST 16'S SEVENTY-FIVE CASUALTIES.

A MESSERSCHMITT WHICH ATTEMPTED TO RAID AN AERODROME.

"THUMBS UP" FOR A VICTORY—"THUMBS DOWN" TO THE SWASTIKA.

to the part played by the ground defences; not only did our anti-aircraft units shoot down 57 bombers and fighters, but they turned back many times that number before they could reach their objective. The Nazi song "Wir Fahren gegen Engelland" must have acquired a somewhat sinister ring in the *Luftwaffe* messes.

*These pages, and pages 242 and 243, joined together form an astonishing panorama of aerial defeat.*

WORLD, S. AND G., PLANET, TOPICAL, FOX, C.P.

were given to WAAF Sergeant Joan Mortimer of Harrogate, Sergeant Helen Turner of London and Corporal Elspeth Henderson of Edinburgh.

Yet despite the German successes on 16 August – successes that, historian Basil Collier believes, 'ought, according to programme, to have put the Luftwaffe within sight of victory' – Kesselring and Sperrle did not press home their advantage and there were no major attacks on Saturday 17 August. It was almost as if the Luftwaffe was taking a traditional English weekend off. And in typical idiosyncratic fashion, in England a cricket match was played at Lord's, while many people once more went off to the tennis courts and golf courses.

Of somewhat more moment, the King took advantage of what he knew was only a lull in the storm to send a personal message of tribute to the RAF. He was, though, certainly speaking on behalf of the nation when he said: 'Please convey my warmest congratulations to the fighter squadrons who in recent days have been so heavily engaged in the defence of our country. I, like all their compatriots, have read with ever-increasing admiration the story of their daily victories. I wish them continued success and the best of luck.'

There was also a chorus of praise for beleaguered Britain in the American newspapers that Saturday morning, where the term 'Battle of Britain' was now being used to describe what was happening across the Atlantic. According to the headline in one paper, the Brits were now 'Putting it over the Heinies!'

The calm and stillness across the nation on Saturday was broken on Sunday morning when shortly after midday the sound of Kesselring's bombers returning to the attack was heard in the skies over southern England. Just as quickly they were joined by the mosquito-like roar of Dowding's Spitfires and Hurricanes. Luftflotte 2's targets this time were the airfields at Biggin Hill, Kenley, Croydon and West Malling; and an hour or so later they were followed by Sperrle's pilots who attacked aerodromes at Thorney Island, Ford and Gosport.

It was not only the British fighter pilots who helped win this crucial day, for in attempting to come in low over the countryside the German pilots ran into a barrage of anti-aircraft guns fired with such speed and accuracy that one enemy officer later described the experience as being like 'flying through a hail of damned rockets'. One Home Guard unit on the outskirts of London, commanded by a First World War army veteran, Captain H.S. Prince, even made history by being the first such group to bring down a German aircraft with rifle fire – a story which, not surprisingly, was prominently featured in the national newspapers the following morning. (The *Daily Mirror*'s typically lively version of this incident, headlined 'Home Guard Bagged Plane at 50ft', is reprinted on page 125.)

As evening fell across Britain that August Sunday, the fresh debris of smouldering German aircraft – each one patrolled by a Home Guard to thwart souvenir hunters – pointed to another good day for the RAF. A final tally showed the Luftwaffe had lost 71 aircraft to Fighter Command's 27. In the four days of intense fighting the previous week, the Germans had sacrificed 236 machines and at least double that many men. The British had lost 95 aircraft, and 94 of their number had been killed or reported missing, with a further 60 wounded. And whereas the two biggest Luftflotten were now desperately awaiting replacement aircraft from Germany, Fighter Command was still at its optimum fighting strength with another 161 Hurricanes and Spitfires immediately available in reserve. The only reserves that Dowding still did not have were fully trained pilots.

Undoubtedly both sides had already paid a high price – though clearly the cost had been far greater to the German Eagle which had singularly failed to crush the resistance of the Fighter Command Sparrow it had been told was already beaten. As Basil Collier has written: 'When the sun went down on August 18, it went down on Goering's chances of doing everything he had set out to do. He had shot his bolt and had failed conspicuously to score.'

There was, however, no cause for celebration or even complacency in England, because as a result of simple pilot error, the nation's cities were about to enter the next phase of the Battle of Britain and experience the hell of *blitzkrieg*.

*'Like flying through a hail of damned rockets' was the German pilots' description of the barrage of fire put up by British anti-aircraft units like this one.*

# WHAT A FOOL!

## Flight Lieutenant J.B. Nicolson Describes the Day He Won a VC

That was a glorious day. The sun was shining from a cloudless sky and there was hardly a breath of wind anywhere. Our squadron was going towards Southampton on patrol at 15,000 feet, when I saw three Junkers 88 bombers about four miles away, flying across our bows. I reported this to our Squadron Leader, and he replied: 'Go after them with your section.' So I led my section of aircraft round towards the bombers. We chased hard after them, but when we were about a mile behind, we saw the 88s fly straight into a squadron of Spitfires. I used to fly a Spitfire myself, and I guessed it was 'curtains' for the three Junkers. I was right, and they were all shot down in quick time, with no pickings for us. I must confess I was very disappointed, for I had never fired at a Hun in my life and was longing to have a crack at them.

So we swung round again, and started to climb up to 18,000 feet over Southampton to rejoin our squadron. I was still a long way from the squadron when suddenly, very close, in rapid succession, I heard four big bangs. They were the loudest noises I had ever heard, and they had been made by four cannon shells from a Messerschmitt 110 hitting my machine. The first shell tore through the hood over my cockpit and sent splinters into my left eye. One splinter, I discovered later, nearly severed my eyelid. I couldn't see through that eye for blood. The second cannon shell struck my spare petrol tank and set it on fire: the third shell crashed into the cockpit and tore off my right trouser leg. The fourth shell struck the back of my left shoe; it shattered the heel of the shoe and made quite a mess of my left foot. But I didn't know anything about that either, until later.

Anyway, the effect of these four shells was to make me dive away to the right to avoid further shells. Then I started cursing myself for my carelessness. What a fool I'd been, I thought – what a fool. I was just thinking of jumping out, when suddenly a Messerschmitt 110 whizzed underneath me and got right in my gun sights. Fortunately no damage had been done to my windscreen and the four sights, and when I was chasing the Junkers I had switched everything off – so everything was set for a fight. I pressed the gun button, for the Messerschmitt was in nice range. He was going like mad, twisting and turning as he tried to get away from my fire, so I pushed the throttle right open. Both of us must have been doing about 400 as we went down together in a dive. First he turned left, then right, then left and right again. He did three turns to the right and finally a fourth turn to the left. I remember shouting out loud at him when I first saw him: 'I'll teach you some manners, you Hun!' – and I shouted other things as well. I knew I was getting him nearly all the time I was firing.

By this time it was pretty hot inside my machine from the burst petrol tank. I couldn't see much flame, but I reckoned it was there all right. I remember looking once at my left hand, which was keeping the throttle open; it seemed to be in the fire itself and I could see the skin peeling off it, yet I had little pain. Unconsciously, too, I had drawn my feet up under my parachute on the seat, to escape the heat, I suppose.

Well, I gave the Hun all I had and the last I saw of him was when he was going down with his right wing lower than the left. I gave him a parting burst, and as he disappeared, I started thinking about saving myself. I decided it was about time I left the aircraft and baled out, so I immediately jumped up from my seat. But first of all I hit my head against the framework of the hood, which was all that was left. I cursed myself for a fool, pulled the hood back . . . and jumped up again. Once again I bounced back into my seat for I had forgotten to undo the straps holding me in; one of them snapped, so I had only three to undo. Then I left the machine. I suppose I was about twelve to fifteen thousand feet when I baled out.

Immediately I started somersaulting downwards and after a few turns like that I found myself diving head first to the ground. After a second or two of this, I decided to pull the rip cord. The result was that I immediately straightened up and began to float down. Then an aircraft (a Messerschmitt, I afterwards heard) came tearing past me. I decided to pretend that I was dead. . . . The Messerschmitt came back once and I kept my eyes closed, but I didn't get the bullets I was half expecting. I don't know if he fired at me – the main thing is that I wasn't hit. When I was about 100 feet from the ground I saw a cyclist and heard him ring his bell. I was surprised to hear the bicycle bell, and realised I had been coming down in absolute silence. I bellowed at the cyclist – but I don't suppose he heard me. Finally I touched down in a field and fell over. Fortunately it was a very calm day. My parachute just floated down and stayed down without dragging me along as they sometimes do. I had a piece of good news almost immediately. One of the people who came along and who had watched the combat said they had seen the Messerschmitt 110 dive straight into the sea. So it hadn't been such a bad day after all.

BBC Radio broadcast
6 September 1940

*Flight Lieutenant James Nicolson winning his VC – a
dramatic reconstruction painted by Norman Clarke
shortly after the pilot's radio broadcast.*

Captain F.H. Clarke, the members of his Home Guard unit, and the Dornier 17 bomber that they brought down with rifle fire on Sunday 18 August.

## HOME GUARD BAGGED PLANE AT
## 50 FEET!

Members of a Home Guard unit who brought down a German dive-bomber with rifle fire hurried home to tell their wives about it – only to be told off because they were late for Sunday dinner.

'Why do these Germans have to come at dinner time? Most inconsiderate. They've spoiled your meal,' was the greeting his wife gave Captain H.S. Prince, one of the sharpshooters, when he arrived home an hour late. But that was before Mrs Prince heard what had happened.

Flying at 400 feet, the plane had opened fire with a machine gun on the Home Guard unit outside its south London headquarters, and then swept down to fifty feet.

The Home Guard blasted back with 180 rounds and saw the plane, belching smoke, flounder away, and crash near a road. It was the first plane to be bagged by the Home Guard.

Most of the members of the unit, which was inspected by the King last week, served in the last war and were only too glad to have another crack at the Germans. When they heard they had scored a bull's eye, they threw their caps in the air and cheered.

'Each man stuck to his post and fired in sections as I called out the orders,' their commanding officer, Captain F.H. Clarke told the *Daily Mirror* yesterday.

Said grey-haired volunteer V.W. Cox, who is 60: 'It was just the opportunity I've been waiting for – wouldn't have missed it for the world.'

'We all had a bit of trouble with our wives afterwards,' said another member of the unit. 'We were late for dinner, you see. But when we explained the reason they were bucked stiff.'

'I'm afraid our boiled beef and dumplings came first with the wife – but I wouldn't have missed the scrap,' added Captain Prince.

*Daily Mirror*
**19 August 1940**

# —8—

# MRS ENGLAND AND MR HITLER'S MISCALCULATION

If there was one thing in the air of Britain on the morning of Monday 19 August it was a spirit of optimism, as typified by the *Daily Mirror*'s headline: 'Business as Usual'. Though the people as they read their papers could not have known that across the Channel, Goering was busy organising the second phase of his assault upon them, they could still enjoy the *Mirror*'s cheering prose.

'The spirit of Britain's womanhood can't be beaten, won't be beaten,' declared the biggest-selling tabloid in the nation, alongside a graphic photograph of a bomb-wrecked street. It continued: 'Bombers came over during the weekend. They dropped their bombs. You see what they did to these houses in a south-western suburb of London. But it won't make any difference to the routine of the British housewife.

'On Monday morning she carries on with the job she's done every Monday morning since she has been a housewife. She does the week's washing. And so, though half the house is open to the skies, Mrs England goes to the washtub in the usual way and gets the washing done.

'And then she hangs out the washing as best she can in what has been left of the garden. And she props up the clothes, while she waits for somebody to prop up her home.'

This resilience, which was uniting the nation through

*Mrs England unbowed! Although her home has been wrecked by one of Hitler's bombs, this mum and her child prepare to carry on with their lives in August 1940.*

the dark hours of the Battle of Britain, was also acknowledged in a leader in *The Times* – though in a rather more formal manner.

'The first phase of the Battle of Britain has ended,' the paper declared. 'It consisted of a very heavy air offensive lasting about a week. The result is not in doubt, but it is possible that we do not even yet realise the extent of our victory. That victory was won by the Fighter Command well supported by anti-aircraft batteries, searchlights, balloon barrages, the counter action of bombers and ARP services.'

And *The Times* added: 'It was, as we do well to remember, our Hurricanes and Spitfires which stood between our cities and the fates of Warsaw and Rotterdam, because fighter opposition is the most powerful of all forms of defence against the bomber and no other weapon can wholly compensate for the lack of it.'

Perhaps not surprisingly, the Government took advantage of this mood to redouble their campaign of urging people to save money. A new series of advertisements appeared in all the papers with the appeal, 'Hit Back with National Savings!' alongside an illustration of a German bomber crashing in flames.

The nation's resolution during the past week had also earned widespread respect among the free nations of the world, and that Monday morning *The Times* also carried a cable message which it had just received from America. 'All Americans admire Britain's courage and effective defence,' the cable said. 'Many of us are helping all we can.' The message was signed Paul White, Boston, Mass.

By coincidence, the paper carried the news of the first death of an American serving with Fighter Command,

*'Business as Usual' –
despite being damaged
by a German bomb,
this off-licence in Kent
was still open for
custom in August 1940.*

FAGS
&
BEER
WE are
ALL
HERE

Pilot Officer W.M.L. 'Billy' Fiske, the son of a wealthy New York banker, who had flown a Spitfire with No. 601 Squadron based at Tangmere. One of the first Americans to join Fighter Command – and also one of the first fighter pilots to have 'scrambled' on Eagle Day – Fiske had several 'kills' to his credit when he met his fate on 18 August. Trying to guide his damaged Spitfire back to base, he actually managed a belly landing, but at once his plane burst into flames and Fiske later died from his injuries. Though he received no medal for his courage, the young pilot's bravery was commemorated by a stone tablet placed in St Paul's Cathedral, London, which can be seen to this day and bears the epitaph: 'An American citizen who died that England might live'.

While the spirit of Billy Fiske was pervading Britain, Goering on 19 August was planning how he could fulfil Hitler's instructions to subdue Britain ready for invasion within a fortnight of the start of his aerial attacks. A week had now gone by and the enemy was clearly far from broken.

The Reichsmarschall decided to step up the attacks on Fighter Command as soon as the weather was suitable – though all bomber operations were to be heavily protected by fighter escorts, he insisted. In this way, he hoped his superior numbers would break Dowding's forces. Kesselring was to concentrate on the south-east of England by day, with Sperrle attacking factories by night or under cloud cover. The badly mauled Stumpff in Norway was to make plans for an attack on Scottish installations. There were, though, the flamboyant Goering told his commanders, to be *no* attacks on the major cities such as London, Liverpool or Glasgow without his express orders.

It was to be another five days – and getting ever closer to their commander's deadline – before the weather improved sufficiently for Goering's pilots to put the second phase of his operation into effect. In the meantime, intermittent raids upon England continued, making heroes of ordinary folk as well as the brave fighters in the sky.

On the Monday evening, for instance, an old-age pensioner single-handedly extinguished an incendiary bomb which fell on her home in the north-west of England. Only a faded cutting from the *Daily Telegraph* still exists to commemorate the bravery of this unnamed eighty-one-year-old spinster, 'her grey hair singed from the blaze', who the next day was still 'puzzling what all the fuss was about', according to the report.

*Winston Churchill being given a standing ovation after his celebrated speech in the House of Commons on 20 August – a moment of history captured by Terence Cuneo.*

'I live by myself,' the old lady is quoted as saying, 'so when I heard a bang in the bedroom next to me I got up to see what had happened. The bedroom was blazing, so I got some rugs and put them on top of the bomb. Then I put a piece of carpet on, too.

'I hurried downstairs, filled a bucket and threw the water on. Then I got three or four more buckets. And the bomb seemed to go out. Still, I went to rouse the neighbours in case there were any more bombs lying around.'

A teenage boy, whose name again is not given, displayed similar bravery the following day according to another report in the *Daily Mail*. 'Boy Helps in Capture', the paper headlined its story, and the text read: 'A 14-year-old boy helped his mother to capture a German airman near a south-east village when a Dornier bomber was brought down by fighters. Two of the crew gave themselves up to farm workers, and the third surrendered when the woman ran up to him followed by the boy who was brandishing his father's Home Guard rifle.'

Equally courageous was the action of a bank clerk in a town close to the south coast who saw a German bomber skim some trees and crash into a field near his home. As the man began to run towards the crash, he saw a figure with a parachute descending towards him. Reaching the middle of the field he waited for the German to land, caught him by the legs, and arrested him!

Such heroism – and that of the pilots of Fighter Command, of course – deservedly earned the memorable recognition that Winston Churchill provided when he stood before a packed House of Commons on Tuesday 20 August to give what had been heralded as the first 'progress report' on the war since the fall of France. Never a man to disappoint his audience, the Prime Minister gave undoubtedly his most rousing speech of the entire war – that which produced the immortal phrase which has rung down through the years, 'Never in the field of human conflict has so much been owed by so many to so few '

Well known though much of this famous speech still is, there are at least two sections less familiar which fifty years on throw an interesting light on Britain at this crucial moment in her history. The first is Churchill's allusion to the state of the nation and the will of the people. 'The fronts are everywhere,' he said. 'Every village is fortified. Every road. The front line runs through the factories. The workmen are soldiers with different weapons but the same courage. These are great and distinctive changes from what many of us saw in the struggle of a quarter of a century ago. . . . If it is a case of the whole nation fighting and suffering together, that ought to suit us, because we entered the war upon the national will and with our eyes open, and because we have been nurtured in freedom and individual responsibility and are the products, not of totalitarian uniformity, but of tolerance and variety.'

The Prime Minister also revealed the extent to which RAF bombers had been supplementing the rear-guard action of the fighters by hitting back at military targets in Germany with considerable effect.

'All our hearts go out to the fighter pilots whose brilliant actions we see with our own eyes day after day,' Mr Churchill said. 'But we must never forget that all the time, night after night, month after month, our bomber squadrons travel far into Germany, find their targets in the darkness by the highest navigational skill, aim their attacks, often under the heaviest fire, often with serious loss, with *deliberately careful discrimination* [my italics], and inflict shattering blows upon the whole of the technical and war-making structure of the Nazi power. And on no part of the RAF does the weight of war fall more heavily than on the daylight bombers who will play an invaluable part in the case of invasion and whose unflinching zeal it has been necessary in the meanwhile on numerous occasions to retrain.'

Reading these words even today, it comes as no surprise that when he sat down the Prime Minister was cheered to the rafters. But no one could have realised just *how* soon the missions of these bombers were to be switched from purely military objectives to civilian targets.

It was just after noon on the following Saturday, 24 August, that England felt the brunt of a massed German attack by Kesselring's Luftflotte 2. As usual there was no panic when the air-raid sirens wailed out their message for the population to take cover – indeed, most people shrugged their shoulders resignedly and strolled calmly into their Anderson shelters.

In London itself, the wail of sirens unexpectedly created a little bit of cricketing history when they brought about a case of 'raid stopped play'. The umpires and teams left the field at Lord's immediately the siren was heard, though quite a few spectators remained in their seats. After all, the heart of London *had* remained unscathed so far! One spectator, a venerable old Chelsea Pensioner resplendent in his red coat, actually walked out to the square to inspect the wicket. When politely asked to go to a shelter by a member of the ground staff, the Old Redoubtable explained that he was only satisfying himself that the wicket would not break up before the other team had a chance to bat!

The first German strike of the second phase of the Battle of Britain proved more of a success than any of their earlier operations. Five Luftwaffe formations of bombers and fighters reached Manston in Kent, and though they lost five Dorniers and two Messerschmitts in combat with the Hurricanes and Defiants sent up to

*The inaccuracy of German bombers led to many tragic incidents. This rural school was fortunately empty when a bomb fell on it, but an old lady in the adjoining house was killed by the blast.*

repel them, the Germans damaged the airfield so badly that it thereafter had to be abandoned as a fighter base.

Following this, Kesselring attacked two other important airfields in Essex, at Hornchurch and North Weald, and it was as much the effort of the anti-aircraft gunners on the ground as the fighter pilots that saved both stations from the same fate as Manston. As in the earlier engagement, the men of Fighter Command found the bombers with their heavy fighter cover much more difficult to approach closely enough to attack.

In the meantime, Sperrle had despatched a force of fifty bombers to raid Portsmouth, and though countered by three squadrons of British fighters over the Isle of Wight, most still reached their destination. The Germans' accuracy was seriously at fault, however, and more damage was done to the town than the factories and harbour, the intended targets. As dusk fell, the Luftwaffe was counting losses of 38 aircraft, while Fighter Command had lost 22.

In previous weeks, the coming of nightfall had signalled the end of major attacks, and doubtless expecting the same this Saturday night, the people of England were soon found enjoying an evening out at the pictures or the theatre, or quietly with friends at a pub or restaurant. However, their relaxation was noisily and rudely interrupted when, on Goering's instructions for round-the-clock bombing, 170 bombers crossed the night skies of Britain to attack targets not only in the south-east, but north to Wales and the Midlands and even as far as South Shields.

From this German force, about a dozen of the bombers had been detailed to attack the aircraft factories at Rochester and Kingston and the oil refineries at Thames Haven. For some reason – whether wilful disregard of Goering's orders *not* to bomb London, or perhaps because they were not sure of their exact location in the profound darkness over blacked-out England – the crews released their payloads over the capital city itself. For the very first time since 1918, London felt the impact of bombs on its busy thoroughfares and tightly packed buildings. Londoners who had been escaping from the war with a little entertainment on the screen or stage emerged to find themselves in the middle of a real nightmare.

At that moment the complexion of the war between Germany and Britain was changed irrevocably. It was, as the *New York Times* later declared, 'One of the greatest miscalculations in history' – for hardly had the dead and wounded been taken from their shattered homes in the East End and at least nine other London districts, than Churchill ordered a retaliatory raid on Berlin for the very next night.

A force of 81 bombers including Wellingtons and Hampdens – the largest that Bomber Command had ever despatched – duly carried out their mission despite heavy cloud over the German capital, and had precisely the same impact upon the civilian population. An enraged Hitler, without bothering to investigate the rights and wrongs of the initial cause of the raid, saw this as the justification he needed for unrestricted

*Following the Luftwaffe's decision to begin night raids from Saturday 24 August, the hard-pressed Fighter Command pilots were soon flying round-the-clock missions; it also meant longer hours for RAF ground staff such as the sergeant* (right) *lighting runway flares for returning aircraft.*

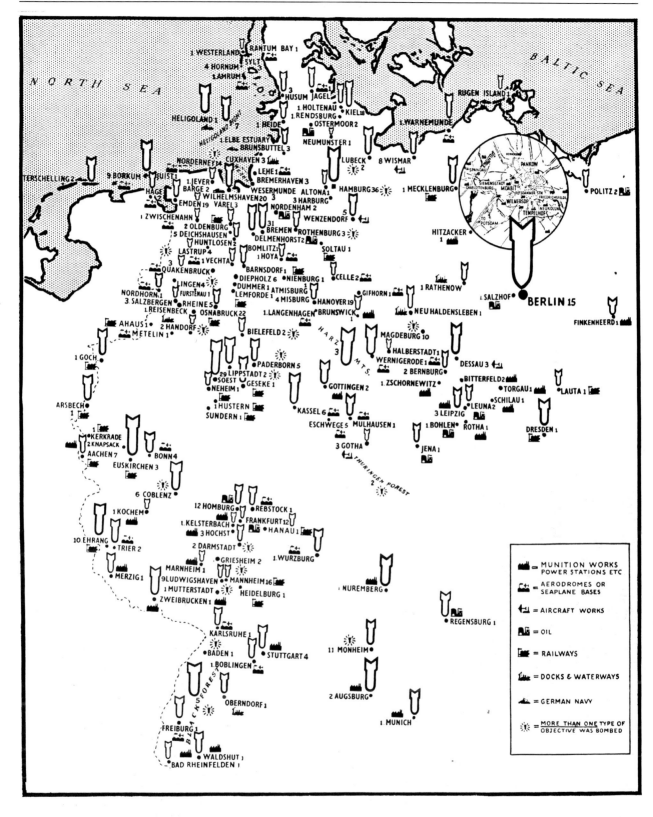

*An official Air Ministry photograph taken from a British bomber of an early retaliatory raid against Germany; and (above) an official RAF map detailing the bombing offensive against Germany up to 30 September 1940. The size of the bomb symbol indicates the intensity of the attack.*

and bloody attacks on the major British cities. From here on he was far less interested in the destruction of air bases and military installations than in the levelling of the great centres of population. But if the Fuehrer had imagined for one moment that such slaughter would bring the British to their knees, he soon learned that on the contrary, it served only to harden their resolve.

The feelings of the majority of the British public about the raid on Berlin were probably best expressed by the leader column in the *Daily Mirror* of 27 August which was headlined: 'Bomb Back'. 'The best defence is offence,' the paper thundered, 'in the air, as on the land and the sea. In this latest phase of the air war, the best defence of our towns and countryside has been the bombing of the Berlin area. The best news for days past.'

And with an eye on what undoubtedly lay ahead, the paper continued: 'We must talk rudely to our raid-gazers, roof-squatters (with cigarettes), our speeding and perpetually gyrating motorists who make noises like air-raid warnings. We must secure uniform, rigid rules about traffic stopping or moving during raids. We must ensure that all shelters be unlocked – for is there much to steal in a shelter, and is a shelter a strong box?

'Then, having done our part, we must go on keeping calm, and hope that as many of our splendid airmen as possible may be set free to get Berliners into their shelters with Gestapo agents sitting on their chests!'

To the political and military reasons for defying Hitler, had now been added the more basic human emotion of anger, enflamed by stories of innocent, crushed bodies in the heart of London. The leader columns in more than one newspaper had begun that week in August maintaining that, thanks to the RAF, 'The Tide is Turning'. Five days on it was the spilling of English civilian blood that was to help force it back with still greater determination.

*An example of the level of damage caused to homes struck by incendiary bombs in the summer of 1940.*

# A BOMB IN THE HOUSE

## John Easton Recounts a Narrow Escape

I never dreamt the Germans would come all that way to drop an incendiary bomb down my cupboard. We had all got the ARP leaflets and the wireless was always calling out about it, telling us what we should do if it happened. The night before the Missus was at the pictures and saw a film demonstrating the stirrup pump, but we hadn't any stirrup pump or buckets of sand or water or anything ready. We just didn't think it would happen.

Me and the Missus was listening to the wireless when the warning came. The two youngest were in a room by themselves; one is six and the other rising eight; on the other side of the room from their bed there is a cupboard where the Missus keeps shoes and linen and some suits hanging up. I went down to the foot of the stair to see what was happening. The searchlights were out and we could hear the drone of an aeroplane very high up. After a bit we heard three big thuds away to south and I came back up the stair and said to the Missus, 'I'm afraid that's a German plane.' I went down the stair again and immediately we hears the plane coming back. All at once the place was lit up with incendiary bombs falling on the countryside.

The plane turned and I imagined that it was going to pass right over the top of the house. I never heard nothing fall. The next thing was I heard the Missus calling to the son that the house was on fire. I really thought that she'd seen the lights through the window and I came up the stair to pacify her by my way of it – and then I found the house was on fire right enough. The bomb had come right through the roof and into the cupboard in the room where the weans were. It was sizzing just like a kiddie's squib. The Missus had opened the cupboard door but she had the presence of mind to shut it again. Her and the son got the two wee ones out and the neighbour from in a-below us had them safe in bed before they were wakened.

'While they were doing that I went through to the living room. I lifted the window and called for assistance. I came back along the passage and heard the neighbours coming up the stairs. John – that's my eldest son – opened the cupboard door. The shoes were all burning by this time and a cardboard box and the suits as well. I went into the bathroom for water and as I was drawing it one of the neighbours cried out: 'Run to the garden for earth.' I brought the bucket of water into the room and John took it from me and jumped on the bed and threw it on the bomb. The bomb seemed to fly right out of the cupboard across the room in a shower of sparks. I shouted to John to come out of there, but by that time somebody else had handed him a bucket of earth and he threw it on. The young lad was lucky not to get himself burnt. If we had put on the water with a spray it would have been all right. As it was, the bedclothes was all smouldering and the linoleum, too. I can tell you that's the last time I'll try to put out one of they bombs with a pail of water.

However, the neighbours brought up earth from the garden and we had it under control before the ARP men arrived with the stirrup pump. We rolled up all the bedclothes and heaved them outside. The fire was still smouldering in the bolster and the mattress a long time after. If we'd put them in another room the house would still have been on fire. I know now, of course, that they need never have been set on fire. If we'd used earth or sand the bomb would never have spread. So we've taken the ARP men's advice now and we've got a bucket of sand ready for next time. We hope there won't be a next time, but we're not taking any chances.

BBC Radio broadcast
23 August 1940

A civilian emerges smiling and unhurt from his Anderson shelter while all around is in ruins.

# LIFE UNDER THE AIR RAIDS

Bed at 6 o'clock is becoming a habit in some north country homes for grown-ups as well as children. In one area at least scarcely a night has passed these last three weeks without either an air raid or an alarm or both, and people have become so used to the nightly disturbance that housewives shop early, prepare the evening meal and get the family off to bed for a spell of sleep before the sirens sound.

If the enemy hope to induce fatigue and despondency by interrupting the rest of the workers, they would learn better from the women here; one of them gave the answer quite simply, 'What sleep I lose won't kill me,' and she told me how the women used to sing their menfolk off to work before others had stirred, and were not going to be beaten by shortened nights.

The men are equally resolved; many sleep partly dressed and are instantly ready to rouse their families and neighbours on the first wail of the siren. They have been working at war speed during the day and one would have expected to find signs of resentment that sleep should have been disturbed. 'We can stand this not for three weeks or three months but for three years if need be,' said one.

This ready recommendation is typical of the way the public is responding to air raids. It will do any 'quakers' – those people who are waiting for their first air raid and fearing what it will be like – good to join the parties in the street shelters. The bairns, far from being terrified, are the least affected of all. They delight in the midnight picnics, the biscuits and hot drinks. And when it is all over they join in singing hymns and songs.

There are no signs of panic in 'Home, Sweet Home', and neighbours are sharing brick-built shelters in the street. Yet it is not many nights since a bomb exploded within a hundred yards of the spot.

Some shopkeepers in the vicinity have even put in new window panes on the theory, apparently, that lightning never strikes twice in the same place; others are boarded up, leaving small grated windows. But all have kept open, rivalling one another in producing the wittiest notice, such as, 'Our business is hit – but not our reputation.'

In another town after a raid, a woman said, 'We were singing and talking in the shelter when we heard some thuds. We little realised that it was our own house that had gone! Now we shall have to go somewhere else to live, but we have still got our chins up and we shall win out.'

Another story is told of a local Francis Drake who went off to play a heat in his club bowling championship without waiting for the 'All Clear' – although a bomb had been dropped in the next street. Such stories can be repeated in many towns, and with the knowledge that no damage of national importance has been done, the calm and confidence of the people are explained.

*Manchester Guardian*
**21 August 1940**

—9—

# A HOT TIME IN THE OLD COUNTRY TONIGHT . . .

Sunday 25 August 1940 is remembered by those who were alive at the time as one of the warmest and most glorious days of that summer. It might almost have been a hint from nature that hot days lay ahead for the nation – and not just as far as the weather was concerned. For, as historian Angus Calder later wrote: 'When the end of the spell of cloudy weather permitted the Luftwaffe to resume heavy attacks, from August 24, it adopted new tactics. By constant patrols over the Channel and by feint attacks to baffle the radar system, it confused and wore down the defences, and was able to punish very severely the vital ring of seven sector stations, the key to the defence of London. In the next fortnight, Britain came very near to losing the battle.'

One man who remembered that Sunday particularly vividly was Lieutenant Colonel C.C. Merritt, a Canadian lawyer who served in the South Saskatchewan Regiment and won a VC at Dieppe. He was in England with his regiment while the battle was raging in the skies above. He has recalled what proved the start of a week of almost constant German attacks, in the following evocative words.

'It was noon and the day was very hot. As we drove into Edenbridge, the streets were almost empty and the warm, peaceful drowsiness of a Kent village was good to look upon. Then suddenly there came the wail of an air-raid siren – at once mournful and strident – and it seemed

*On a cloudless August day, two observers keep watch over London for any sign of German raiders. These men were nicknamed 'Jim Crows'.*

particularly discordant in that lovely scene.

'Even as we climbed out of our car we heard shouts of "There they are!" from people running out of houses into the streets,' Lt Col Merritt continued. 'And as I looked up, following their gaze, into that cloudless sky with its hot sun blazing down, I saw an unforgettable sight. Right above me, at no great height, a large, closely packed formation of two-motored German bombers was droning its seemingly slow and implacable way in the direction of London. The thought of their capacity for destruction cut sharply across my appreciation of the glint of the sunlight upon their glistening wings.

'I was acutely aware of the vast power behind these determined attempts upon the chief stronghold of fair-dealing and freedom. The skill and dash of those charged with the parrying of these continuous heavy blows inspired me with confidence indeed, but I could not help being oppressed by the comparison between the importance of the issue and the slenderness of the numerical resources of Fighter Command.'

But as the Canadian soldier, who after the war became a leading MP in his native land, recalled, he need not have worried. 'As I looked,' he added, 'I saw some thousand yards behind the bombers, the flash of a section of our fighters diving on their tails and simply eating up the distance between them. There was a sharp rattle above the drone of the motors – the sound of an eight-gun Spitfire. The rearmost bomber turned on its back and plummeted to the ground. Two and then a third white parachute blossomed against the backdrop of the blue sky. Then other fighters joined the action. My vague fears were stilled.'

*Some rural bungalows in eastern England bombed in August 1940.*

# OUR VILLAGE

## RURAL REFLECTIONS AFTER AN AIR RAID

### FROM A CORRESPONDENT

We were awakened the other night, with no warning but two terrific crashes, followed by a deep silence, save for the strange " chug, chug, chug " with which we who have come from a South Coast area have learned (despite General Jourbert) to associate enemy aeroplanes. There was a flare of fire behind a wooded hill, and we heard the raider return twice, I suppose to take back details to Berlin of the damage done to military objectives ; these being one empty house and a barn burned down, and one high-explosive bomb dropped in a ploughed field.

Next morning we went to see the damage. The little village, consisting of about 12 houses, was in high feather at being the unwonted centre of attraction. Visitors were welcomed warmly and directed to a stile, where the oldest inhabitant was stationed to point out the way to " the crater." Arrived there, we found a still older inhabitant leaning on his stick, gazing into the hole. " I could 'a done better myself with a spade," he remarked thoughtfully. " We ought to plant a apple tree to mark the spot," he added.

A cheerful individual was explaining to open-mouthed listeners : " At the first bang I stayed in bed. But at the second—well, I reckon I got up pretty quick. The wife said : ' Let's have a cup o' tea,' so we did. Them little houses down there got their winders broke and a door blown out, and a ceilin's come down, but no one hurt much." A woman holding a shy little girl by the hand said : " Gladys was a bit startled-like at the bang. But I took 'er inter bed with me and she was quite all right, weren't yer, Gladys ? "

Meanwhile, from the most damaged of the little houses came the cheerful sounds of a gramophone. It was evidently considered a great occasion, and one on which a spot of music would be suitable for the visitors. In the tiny shop I found a cheerful old woman selling biscuits. She had lost nearly all her stock of provisions, and was herself, as she proudly informed me, " A minor casualty," some of the ceiling having fallen on her leg. She was even more wreathed in smiles than the others.

Suddenly there was a clapping of hands from the twenty or so villagers who stood by the roadside. A car had drawn up, and out of it emerged a well-known figure, four-square to all the winds that blow. He raised his hat to us, smiled his curious smile, and proceeded to visit the battered shop and speak to one or two of the people. When he got into his car again someone in the crowd shouted " God bless you," and the others took it up. He raised his hand in acknowledgment and drove off.

An old lady of 75 came hurrying out of her cottage next door. " The Prime Minister ! Why didn't he come into my house, too ; its much worse than Mrs. X, and I could have showed him a lot, I could ! " " You see, it is our first air raid," said the vicar's wife, smiling apologetically to us, in allusion to the general cheerfulness.

" Gladys was a bit startled-like," and " the wife made a cup of tea." . . . Hitler has not been up against English homes yet. I fear he is in for a big disappointment.

*In the fields of Kent the harvesting continues in August 1940, while the Army exercises with its long-range guns. The picture is by Captain Bryan de Grineau.*

The Lieutenant Colonel was in actual fact just one of many thousands who witnessed the inexorable progress of the Luftwaffe forces that Sunday afternoon – and in the days that immediately followed – yet all shared his confidence in the ability of Fighter Command and continued to go about their appointed business.

For example, across a considerable swathe of England farmers and their men were taking advantage of the weather to get in the harvest – and making light of any interruptions the Nazi raiders might cause. Mr E.S. Oak-Rhind, the Chairman of the Civil Defence Committee for Kent, recalled watching some harvesters at work

GUNNERY BARRAGES AND HARVESTING
ON THE SOUTH-WEST COAST FARMS.

when a group of raiders suddenly appeared over the horizon.

'I wondered what the men's reactions might be,' he said. 'But even when the sound of the advancing enemy was audible, still the harvest work went on. It was not until our intercepting squadrons roared overhead that there was any change in their manner. Then, as a man, the workers stood upright and still, doffed their caps – then carried on as the battle raged!'

In another Kent village, according to a story in the *Daily Sketch* of the following day, virtually all the inhabitants turned out to help one farmer whose harvesting

was disrupted by a hail of incendiary bombs from the skies. In quick succession, over fifty incendiaries fell on a 30-acre field of barley. 'When the bombs dropped I thought the whole place would go up,' the man told one of the newspaper's reporters. 'But people came running from the village and we tackled the blaze with spades full of earth as quickly as we could. In less than an hour every bomb had been dealt with.' Grateful as the farmer was for all this assistance, he also confessed ruefully that more damage had probably been done by the fire-fighters tramping about among the untouched barley than by the bombs.

*Just two of a number of fallen German raiders put on show in Britain at the end of August 1940 to raise money for Lord Beaverbrook's Spitfire Fund. The photograph (top)* of the Messerschmitt 109 was taken *in Stevenage, Hertfordshire, while the other, of a Messerschmitt 110 being unloaded for display, was taken at Hendon Park in London.*

There are, to be sure, endless similar stories of bravery and resourcefulness shown by people living in the rural districts of England during the summer of 1940, most of which have tended to be overshadowed by the high drama of the raids on London in the autumn. And it is with this in mind that the item 'Our Village – Rural Reflections After an Air Raid' is reprinted in this book. The village in question is not named – but then it does not need to be, for its people and their experiences could be matched in hundreds of similar communities, and it should therefore be read as a reflection of them all.

But to return to the German planes that the people of Kent saw flying over their skies at noon on 25 August. The force consisted of 45 bombers accompanied by more than 200 fighters from Sperrle's Luftflotte 3, and they had

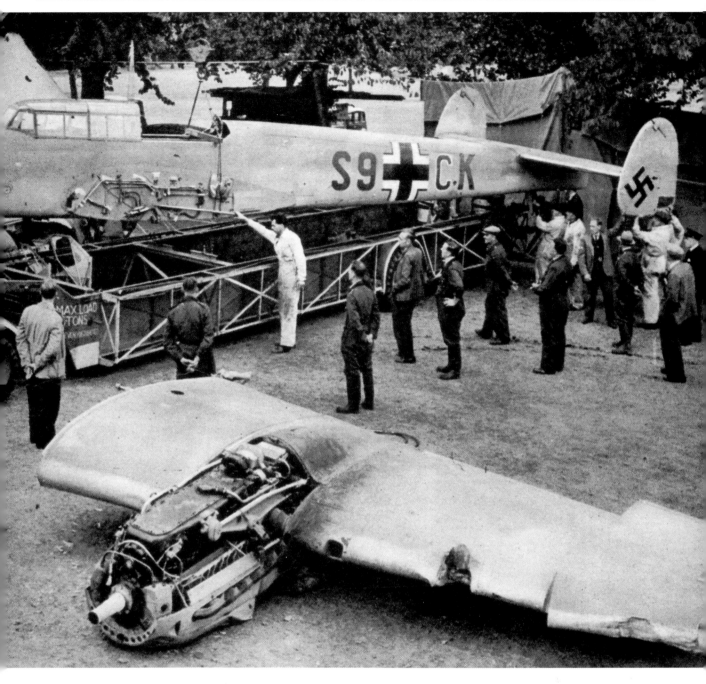

their sights – and bombs – set on one of Fighter Command's important forward bases at Warmwell. Because of the strong fighter cover, Dowding's men were able to destroy only one bomber and the aerodrome was badly damaged. The success of the raid did, though, cost the Germans ten fighters, but the RAF also lost eleven with eight pilots killed or wounded.

There were further German raids on England throughout the night – including the bombing of London as a result of Hitler's angry decision to hit civilian targets – and on Monday, Kesselring's Luftflotte 2 attacked aerodromes in Kent, Essex and Suffolk, again inflicting considerable damage. Only Sperrle's men, who targeted Portsmouth, were rebuffed. Thanks to the ground defences of the 5th Anti-Aircraft Division and three of

Air Vice-Marshal Park's squadrons, the large force of Nazi fighters and bombers was unable to drop its bombs on the dockyard, and though some fell on the town, many more were jettisoned at sea.

Portsmouth proved to be the first battle since the beginning of Goering's new phase in which his heavily protected bombers suffered badly, losing a total of 19 machines. At the end of the day 26 German fighters were also accounted for, as compared with 31 of Fighter Command's aircraft. An eye-witness on the ground to this dramatic action was Mr Edward Doran, the MP for North Tottenham, who was visiting the south coast on Parliamentary business, and he described the scene.

'I remember that the sky was suddenly blackened by what appeared to be at least a hundred German machines. Then came our Spitfires and they were in and out of the German group like terriers after mastiffs. The Germans appeared to be thoroughly demoralised and were harassed to such an extent as to be totally incapable of putting up a fight. I saw three of them burst into flames. The others turned tail and ran away, our boys chasing them.'

Mr Doran also felt the need to inject a little philosophy about what he had witnessed. 'One can quite readily see that it is not only the machine that is going to count in this war,' he said. 'It is the men in charge of it, and with all the German boasts about their marvellous *kultur*, Germany never has and never will breed the wonderful type of Britisher who is the envy and admiration of the world. It is a thousand pities that the entire population of Great Britain did not witness what I saw, because had they done so they would have felt not only pride in our Air Force, but would have been encouraged by the knowledge that men of such spirit can never be beaten and that the victory over the German scourge can now only be a matter of time!'

Even allowing for an MP's natural tendency towards overstatement, the success of the battle over Portsmouth that Monday afternoon was a welcome boost to the British cause. Coincidentally, it fell exactly at the end of the fortnight Hitler had said he would allow before deciding if the Luftwaffe had progressed far enough in their offensive against England to initiate an invasion. Even to a man as obsessive as the Fuehrer, there was no denying the evidence. The last few days might well have been the most successful in the campaign so far, but Hitler knew he was not ready – yet.

August 27 proved a curiously quiet day, with only a handful of skirmishes over the Channel. In England the newspapers were taken up with a sense of outrage over the machine-gunning of a yacht the previous Saturday, and a long-awaited decision from the Air Ministry about exhibiting crashed German aircraft.

The incident with the yacht had occurred on the Saturday afternoon when a weekend sailor, Colonel J.N. Beddington, relaxing with some friends in his yacht *Orca* about five miles off the Welsh coast, was attacked by two enemy aircraft. The Germans had apparently dived on the craft from out of the blue, the sound of the yacht's diesel motor drowning out their engines until they were almost upon it. Each plane had fired a round of bullets, one burst striking Colonel Beddington and killing him instantly. The planes then disappeared and the remaining members of the crew were able to reach port, although the *Orca* was holed in several places. The unprovoked attack was described in several reports as another example of 'unprovoked German barbarism'.

The other story concerned the Air Ministry, who had been debating for some time whether or not to hold a big exhibition in London of German aircraft shot down in raids over the country. 'It has been decided,' a spokesman for the Ministry was quoted as saying with due solemnity, 'that it is inadvisable to stage anything that would result in large crowds being assembled in limited areas. A number of local exhibitions will, however, be held in various parts of the country.'

In the light of the fury that was to be unleashed on London shortly, this can be seen as a very wise decision.

On Wednesday 28 August Kesselring renewed his attacks on several aerodromes in Kent and Essex, and though unwittingly contributing another 30 aircraft to the Air Ministry's proposed exhibitions, inflicted a lot more damage on Dowding's defences and destroyed 20 of his fighters.

That evening, under specific instructions from Goering, Sperrle initiated the first of four successive night attacks on Merseyside. Despatching on average fleets of 150 long-range bombers, the Germans flew over 600 sorties at the cost of just 7 bombers. In all they unleashed 455 tons of high explosives and 1000 canisters of incendiaries. Although their accuracy was still poor – some raiders hit targets as far away as the Midlands and Tyneside! – and the raids achieved very little from a tactical point of view, their bombs were responsible for hundreds of fires across the northern countryside. The British newspapers, anxious not to shake morale, referred to these sorties as 'nuisance raids' – though they had been a bit more than that to those kept awake all night or disrupted during their vital shift work!

Thursday 29 saw Kesselring hurl more of his fighter planes into swift attacks across the Channel, and although he lost 17 aircraft to Fighter Command's 9, the commander of his organisation, General Kurt von Doring, sweepingly claimed that the Luftwaffe had now attained 'unlimited fighter superiority' over the RAF. Even Hitler in Berlin was not entirely convinced by this statement, but still informed his generals that he would make his decision about the invasion of Britain

*British toy manufacturers took advantage of the increased interest among children in enemy planes in the summer of 1940 to produce new models. In fact, as a result of the war Germany was no longer able to flood the world markets with its models, and British exports increased by 50 per cent, according to this report in the* Illustrated London News *of 24 August 1940. (Interestingly, one of the models of an Army vehicle and the caption referring to it have been obliterated on the orders of the Censor!)*

# TOYS FOR CHILDREN—AND THE R.A.F.:
## BRITAIN EXPORTS "DORNIERS" AND "MESSERSCHMITTS."
SPECIALLY PHOTOGRAPHED FOR "THE ILLUSTRATED LONDON NEWS."

TOY GERMAN AEROPLANES, MANY OF WHICH ARE BOUGHT BY THE R.A.F. FOR TRAINING AIRMEN IN IDENTIFICATION. A MESSERSCHMITT "109" (LEFT) AND A DORNIER "215."

A BARRAGE BALLOON, WITH ITS ATTENDANT WAGON AND TRAILER PILED WITH HYDROGEN CYLINDERS: A BRITISH TOY FOR EXPORT.

(LEFT TO RIGHT, FRONT ROW) SEARCHLIGHT LORRY, BREAKDOWN LORRY, ▓▓▓▓▓▓▓▓▓▓▓▓ SIX-WHEEL ARMY LORRY, ARMY CANVAS-TILT LORRY. (2ND ROW) FORD STAFF CAR, VAUXHALL STAFF CAR, TRANSPORT VAN, LUTON TRANSPORT VAN. (3RD ROW) "WHIPPET" TANK, ARMY PETROL LORRY, MEDIUM TANK, HEAVY TANK. (4TH ROW) ARMY TRACTOR, MEDIUM TRACTOR AND TRAILER, HEAVY TRACTOR AND TRAILER.

CLOCKWORK TOYS, MOSTLY UNWARLIKE. EXAMPLES OF THE BIG RANGE MANUFACTURED FOR EXPORT BY MESSRS. LINES BROS., NEAR LONDON.

MODEL TANKS, AEROPLANES (INCLUDING A MOST LIFELIKE "LYSANDER"), BARRAGE BALLOONS AND ARMY VEHICLES OF VARIOUS DESCRIPTIONS.

GIRLS AT MESSRS. LINES' FACTORY BUSY ON MODELS OF SOME OF THE LATEST TYPES OF AEROPLANES. THIS IS SAID TO BE THE LARGEST TOY FACTORY IN THE WORLD.

*These houses in a Midlands town were hit by German bombs on the night of Wednesday 28 August. The official target was Merseyside!*

on 10 September, allowing the forces in France ten days to prepare themselves for landings on 21 September between Folkestone and New Romney, Camber Sands and Eastbourne, and Birling Gap and Brighton. Their first objective was to be a line from Brighton to Canterbury by way of Uckfield, Tenterden and Ashford, the Fuehrer said.

While it is certainly *not* true that Goering's air force was in control as August came to an end, nor that the courage and determination of Fighter Command was in any way faltering, the strength of Dowding's men was undeniably dwindling, especially in terms of experienced pilots. There was just no way of replacing them overnight, and not a few were nearing physical exhaustion. A major consolation was, of course, that thanks to all the hard work in the production factories, the reserves of aircraft were still as high as ever, while (although not known at the time) the Germans were struggling to keep pace with the demand for spares and had no organisation to match Beaverbrook's.

But tiredness does not affect just one group of men: across the Channel, the German pilots had also been subjected to an unrelenting series of sorties and were in need of rest, too. And if we are to believe one newspaper story that week, they were in even more desperate straits than their English counterparts. For, according to a *Daily Telegraph* headline, 'Germans Are Shooting Each Other Down!'

'Prompted no doubt by the frequency with which their pilots have been mistaking their own colleagues for enemies and shooting each other down,' the paper reported, 'the Germans are now painting some of their fighters distinctive colours. Some have vivid orange streaks on the wing tips, nose and tail; others have distinctive colouring on the engine cowling, wings and rudder.'

Citing a specific example of the strain the Luftwaffe was evidently now under, the *Telegraph* added: 'Only a day or so ago, a Spitfire pilot was about to attack the nearer of two Messerschmitt 109s, when the second came along and obligingly shot it down!'

That same day *The Times* also carried what it considered a cheering story about a 'new device' which had evidently been fitted into German planes 'in view of the consistency with which our Hurricanes and Spitfires are shooting down Messerschmitts'. The report stated: 'A number of the German fighter aircraft are believed to be now fitted with a spring under the pilot's seat to assist parachute escapes. The spring is apparently released by a button or lever at the side of the pilot's compartment, and is so strong that it hurls the pilot straight out of the cockpit like a Jack-in-the-Box, throwing him clear of the aircraft. A Hurricane pilot who attacked a Messerschmitt 109 a day or so ago saw

his bullets entering the fuselage. "I was surprised to see the pilot spring into the air like a man standing to attention, and then make a parachute landing!"'

No matter how tired the German and British pilots might have felt, their commanders threw them into ever more feverish activity. On 30 August, Fighter Command, believing that the Luftwaffe's fighting and bombing strength had been severely reduced, ordered over 1000 sorties to be flown for the first time during the battle. Kesselring, similarly believing the British strength to be waning fast, launched attacks on aerodromes in Kent and the Vauxhall factory making aircraft parts at Luton. Biggin Hill, the famous fighter station, was also seriously damaged. The cost to Luftflotte 2 was 36 aircraft, and to Fighter Command 26.

It was a day of surprises for both sets of pilots, in particular the Germans who had been assured that the battle was all but won. Perhaps, though, the biggest surprise of all was that suffered by the crew of a Dornier bomber who found themselves suddenly rammed by a Hurricane whose pilot, Flight Lieutenant E.J. Morris, then calmly baled out of his machine. Morris parachuted safely to the ground in the wake of the crashing bomber, and on landing became an immediate folk hero. Among the many yarns related about him in the press was the claim that he had deliberately rammed the German raider when his guns became jammed!

The most significant fact on that last Friday of the month was the now greater proximity to London of the battle – a fact reflected in the newspaper headlines on Saturday morning. The *Daily Mirror*, for one, ran a headline in two-inch high letters: 'LONDON RAIDERS CRASH IN SUBURBS', and underneath in bold type reported: 'Fierce air battles raged over the London area yesterday, when the enemy made three daylight bids in force to pierce London's defences. Bombs were dropped, killing several people and damaging industrial plant. At least 54 enemy planes are known to have been downed in the three raids – ten of these in the London area during the third warning.' (A selection of the news items from the *Mirror*'s extensive coverage of the day is included in the panel, 'Fight by Fight' on page 154.)

The figures of enemy aircraft destroyed were clearly being exaggerated in the press and on the radio, but there could be no denying that Goering's pilots were getting ever closer to the heart of the nation. And indeed, as the people of London began clearing the rubble that weekend they had good reason for wondering just how long it would be before they and their homes would become the *actual* rather than the accidental target of those bombers growing ever larger in numbers and more ominous in the skies above.

# FIGHT BY FIGHT

One air battle between the German raiders and our fighters not far from London looked like a trapeze act according to eye-witness Harry Wainwright. He said:

'The RAF fighters zoomed and dived and the bombers made frantic efforts to keep in formation. They failed. One was detached.

'This Jerry knew he was trapped, and he circled madly round and round in a bid to dodge a fighter which was marking him, while two other fighters flew out of my sight on the tail of a pair of other Germans.

'Then the fighter pilot, timing his dive magnificently, swooped in for the kill. There was the rat-tat-tat of bullets, the flare from the tracers, and – whoops! – it was all over, with smoke pouring from the bomber as it dived to the ground.'

Mrs Betty Oliver, who lives on the high ground above the London area, said: 'We saw a formation of German machines tearing across the sky like silver arrows darting about. They were being chased.

'Then we ran into the scullery and looked through the window. They went over almost on top of our house, and one of our fighters was directly over the German. In an instant that silver-looking plane was diving to the ground, with its tail in flames.'

Home Guard Tom Barton also saw the raiders overhead from his post on the outskirts of London.

'I saw a German plane swooping towards us, followed by a Spitfire pouring burst after burst into it. At first we thought the Jerry was going to crash right down on top of us.

'But the pilot seemed to make a supreme effort – and although he was down to about 30 feet from the ground managed to pull his machine over a stationary train full of passengers. Before the plane crashed two of the crew baled out. For a time the area around us seemed to be full of crashing German machines.'

A passenger on the stationary train, Mrs Doris Beckett, who was travelling home from the city during the raid, said:

'Our train was just outside a railway station when a German bomber skimmed the top of the carriages. How it missed us I don't know. There were flames bursting from its tail.

'The bomber skimmed the house-tops, bounced on a children's playground (which was fortunately empty), fell into a road thirty feet below, then bounced high into the air, eventually crashing into a tree and stopping about twenty yards from a shelter crowded with people.

'When the people on the train saw the machine burst into flames they were so thrilled that they cheered!'

*Daily Mirror*
**31 August 1940**

*A remarkable sketch made by BBC News reporter Robin Duff at Hyde Park Corner, London, when a Spitfire destroyed a Dornier 17. The main part of the aircraft crashed near Victoria Station.*

# —10—

# THE GRAVEYARD OF ENEMY DREAMS

The first anniversary of the declaration of war against Germany was to coincide with Goering's order to his men to begin the bombing of London. Hitler, who was smarting under the damage done to his prestige with the citizens of Berlin whom he had assured that no enemy would ever threaten from the sky, bluntly told the commander of the Luftwaffe to 'exterminate British cities'. He announced the news publicly – and predictably – in a speech given at the Sportspalast in Berlin on 4 September, following the decision he had made probably as early as 30 August. The Fuehrer thundered: 'When the British Air Force drops two or three or four thousand kilograms of bombs, then we will drop in one night 150, 250, 300 or 400 thousand kilograms! When they declare that they will increase their attacks on our cities, then we will raze their cities to the ground! We will stop the handiwork of these night air pirates, so help us God!'

And, pausing for the welcome applause from his live audience to die down, he added: 'In England they're filled with curiosity and keep asking, "Why doesn't he come?" Be calm. He's coming. He's *coming*!'

Hitler ordered that British cities were to be harassed by day *and* night – though in the next breath he turned down a plan from one of his more radical generals to bomb indiscriminately residential districts, in favour of striking at military objectives. Perhaps, it might be argued, there was still an ounce of compassion existing in his soul – though the fact of the matter was that bombing by night was still such an inaccurate science (as Sperrle's pilots had discovered when raiding Merseyside) that *anywhere* in the vicinity was likely to be hit!

In any event, while Hitler determined to go after the British hide, in another typical display of idiosyncrasy a grand fashion show of fur coats for export was being held in London! A report in *The Star* of 31 August reported

matter-of-factly: 'A mannequin display of fur coats shortly to be sent to Canada by the British Fur Trade Export Group was held in London yesterday. It was opened by Sir Cecil Wear, executive member of the Export Council, on behalf of the Board of Trade.

'The parade which followed was confined as far as possible to empire furs and was based on practicability and selling price. The collection, which represents fur coats to the value of £100,000 which are immediately available for export, will be shown in Montreal, Toronto, Winnipeg, Hamilton and Quebec.'

Such a report probably did little more than raise a few eyebrows amidst the more important issues of the day. It certainly caught nothing like the attention of another announcement – that, as from Monday 2 September, a new insurance policy was being launched to cover men, women and children killed or injured in air raids. The scheme, known as the 'Thousand-to-one Air Raid Insurance', was to be available to any member of the public on payment of a monthly premium of one shilling (the equivalent of five pence). In the event of an air raid, if a person was killed, lost both eyes, two limbs, or an eye and a limb, the sum of one thousand shillings (or £50) would be paid to them or their dependants.

According to the widespread coverage the policy received in the press, the only people excluded from the scheme would be members of the three Services and the auxiliary bodies. Home Guards could take out the insurance, but it would apply only when they were off duty. 'Already,' said a *Daily Sketch* article, 'considerable

*Another raider for the graveyard! An ME 109, which crashed in Windsor Great Park while diving on British aircraft, being hauled away to be turned into scrap.*

AN R.A.F. FIGHTER CAN CLAIM A DEFINITE VICTIM WITHOUT FURTHER PROOF IF HE SEES HIS OPPONENT GO DOWN IN FLAMES.

—OR, FOLLOWING HIS ANTAGONIST DOWN HE SEES HIM HIT THE GROUND.

—OR SEES HIM CRASH INTO THE SEA.

*Two interpretations of the Battle of Britain statistics.*
*(above) The RAF's rules for claiming a 'kill', and (right)*
*a humorous comment by another famous* Punch
*cartoonist, 'Pont'.*

numbers of people and large works all over the country are taking up the scheme!'

The enthusiasm for this insurance policy had doubtless been fired by the announcement that civilian casualties in air raids during the month of August had included 1075 killed. Some other equally revealing, though less grim, statistics were also published as the second year of the war began. During the previous twelve months, it was stated, the pilots of Fighter Command had flown more than 17 million miles – the equivalent to 700 times around the world. This huge mileage had, however, been built up almost solely by short flights – the great majority of them being of less than an hour's duration.

In September 1939, Dowding's men had flown just 200,000 miles and had not shot down a single enemy aircraft over or near Britain. And even by the end of December their total mileage had not reached 500,000 miles. Yet, despite the fact that January and February had seen some of the hardest weather for over forty years, during that period the Spitfires, Hurricanes and other fighters had clocked up 1,750,000 miles. In March, while mainly patrolling the North Sea to protect shipping and fishing fleets, the pilots had flown 1,700,000 miles. Since then, added the report from the Ministry of Information, the mileage had risen steadily month by month to a peak of 4,500,000 during August.

Not surprisingly, no let-up in the increases was predicted – though the report was happy to conclude, 'Last month was also a record month for victories. During the very many flights over and around our shores our fighters accounted for 964 bombers and fighters.'

A little simple arithmetic from the figures quoted on earlier pages of this book will show that this total is somewhat exaggerated. But what reader back in 1940 could be bothered with such niceties when it was clear from the statistics what a remarkable contribution the boys in blue

*" But you must remember that I outnumbered them by one to three."*

'Operation Cromwell': a rare photograph of a Home Guard unit in Sussex putting the anti-invasion plans into effect to prevent German air- and sea-borne troops from overrunning the country on Saturday 7 September.

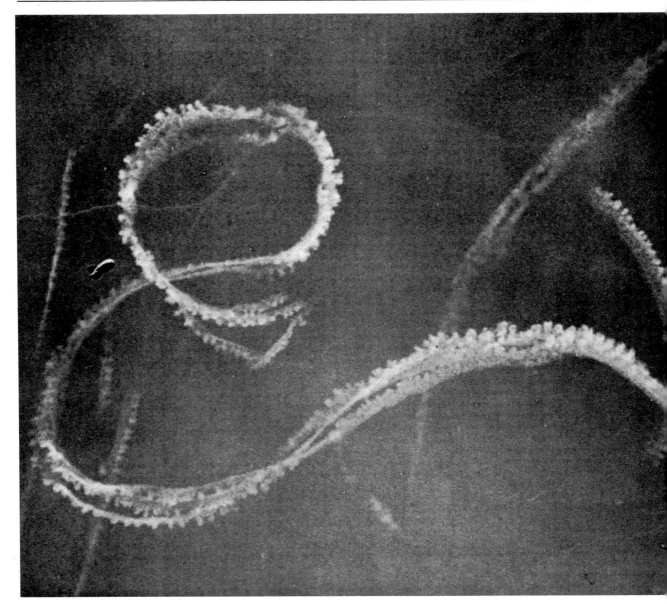

*Fighter Command on the brink:* (above) *a criss-cross of lines trace the course of a desperate duel between British and German fighter planes as seen from the ground;* (right) *a Hurricane with its rudder and tail almost shot away just makes it back to base with a belly landing.*

were making to the war against Germany?

Lord Beaverbrook also took the opportunity of the anniversary to congratulate the nation on its generosity to the Spitfire Fund. 'It will help us to make the sky of Britain a graveyard of our enemy's dream of victory,' he said, with a turn of phrase that was worthy of Churchill. 'And under its wings we shall find certain protection against the tyranny that threatens us all.'

The Minister of Aircraft Production must have allowed himself a smile when he heard about one particular donation which had been made that weekend. A German pilot, shot down over Kent, had donated a five-mark note to the fund! The man was being escorted under armed guard by train through Chatham when the train had pulled up with his compartment opposite a refreshment buffet. A waitress had held out her Spitfire Fund collecting box to the pilot and, when he understood what it was for, asked one of his guards for his wallet, which had been confiscated. 'Smilingly, he pushed a note

into the box,' said the *News Chronicle*'s account of the event. 'It has been suggested that the note should be auctioned for the fund.'

The pilot was just one of a large number of Germans – 41 in all – who had been shot down on 31 August, the fiercest day of fighting so far. Kesselring had redoubled his attacks on aircraft factories and oil refineries, as well as bombing major Fighter Command airfields in Essex, Cambridge, Surrey and Kent, causing considerable devastation.

Biggin Hill, in particular, directly on the line to London, was a target six times over a period of three days, which left it almost wrecked and having suffered the loss of almost a hundred personnel. Just how important it was for this station to remain operational was later expressed by Air Vice-Marshal Park. 'Had the enemy continued his heavy attacks against Biggin Hill and the adjacent sectors,' he said, 'and knocked out their operations rooms or telephone communications, the fighter

## A WARNING TO WARDENS

### John Betjeman Talks About Changes in the Countryside

There have been many changes in our countryside of late. The removal of those hideous tin signs of place-names, for instance, while conversely the rumble of iron-rimmed cartwheels has taken the place of the endless gear-changing of motor cars, now thankfully garaged by petrol rationing.

One particular sound we will miss in the country are church bells: the mellow lin-lan-lone across the hay. And here I would like to put in a word of advice. If any country air raid warden thinks he is going to be able to ring the church bells as a warning of invasion, let him be sure he knows how to handle a bell.

I picture to myself an excited warden running up the belfry stairs, giving a colossal pull at a bell-rope, and finding himself either hauled up to the belfry roof and crashing down unconscious on the floor with his skull cracked open, or else I see him with skin ripped off his hands as the bell rope slides through it, or else I see him hanged by the neck as the rope end coils itself round him!

Bell-ringing is an art, and I wonder how many country wardens have learnt it? As this is not a talk on bell-ringing, and I have not the time to tell you how to ring a church bell, I beg all wardens who contemplate ringing to consult a ringer immediately.

BBC Radio broadcast
4 September 1940

*The 'Gadget King', W. Heath Robinson, created this modified motorcycle as a wartime aid for Wardens in September 1940.*

defences of London would have been in a perilous state during the last critical phase when heavy attacks were directed against the capital.'

No less a figure than the Prime Minister himself confirmed this judgement. 'In the fighting between 24 August and 6 September, the scales had tilted against Fighter Command,' Winston Churchill later wrote. 'During these crucial days the Germans had continuously applied powerful forces against the airfields of south and south-east England. Their object was to break down the day fighter defence of the capital which they were impatient to attack. Far more important to us than the protection of London from terror-bombing was the functioning and articulation of the airfields and the squadrons working from them. In the life-and-death struggle of the two Air Forces this was a decisive phase.

'It was therefore with a sense of relief that Fighter Command felt the German attack turn to London on 7 September, and concluded that the enemy had changed his plan. Goering should certainly have persevered against the airfields, on whose organisation and combination the whole fighting power of our Air Force at this moment depended. By departing from the classical principles of war, as well as from the hitherto accepted dictates of humanity, he made a foolish mistake.'

Goering, it was clear, was about to miss his last and greatest chance of victory.

As it was, the last day of August ended on an extraordinary note of camaraderie between men who were supposed to be deadly enemies. However the leaders of the fighter pilots might rant against one another – and however critical the danger to England might be – there was still room for humanity to surface from time to time.

The incident in question had followed a battle over Kent in which a Hurricane pilot had downed two Messerschmitts and then suddenly seen a third ME 109 flash by him. Although the Englishman was now out of ammunition, he decided to tail the invader.

'I followed him down to ground level and chased him southwards,' the unnamed pilot was quoted as saying in the *Daily Express*. 'He did not rise above 100 feet until well south of Maidstone and then he throttled back. I overtook him and flew alongside him, pointing downwards to the ground. He turned away and so I carried out a dummy quarter attack, breaking away very close to him. After this he landed his ME 109 in a field at about 140 mph.

'I saw the pilot get out apparently unhurt, and as I circled round him he put his hands above his head, so I waved to him and he waved back. Then I circled low over him and threw a packet of 20 cigarettes which I had with me. I saw him pick them up and again he waved. Then I saw what I believed to be members of the Home Guard go into the field and take him prisoner. After that I returned to my base.'

This pilot was one of the lucky ones: Fighter Command lost 39 aircraft in combat that day, as well as at least a dozen Spitfires destroyed on the ground before they could take off. Although the Luftwaffe had suffered just as badly, the situation was now critical at a number of the air bases vital to the protection of London, and on 1 September Goering was certainly 'within measurable distance of his goal', to quote Basil Collier.

The Reichsmarschall, however, had to follow his leader's instructions and initiate a new phase of operations in which Kesselring was to devote his forces to attacking London by day and Sperrle to bomb it by night. He hoped that Dowding would then throw all his fighter resources – both those that were operational and whatever he might have in reserve – into defending the precious capital, and could thus be driven from the sky once and for all.

Totting up his aerial armada, Goering learned that Luftflotte 3 now consisted of 300 bombers, while Luftflotte 2 could muster 450. There were some 600 fighters, making a total operational force just in excess of 1300 machines. The impact of Dowding's 'Chicks' upon these numbers can be gauged when one remembers that the Luftwaffe had been more than 2000 aircraft strong on Eagle Day.

Because of the size of London, the Luftwaffe divided it into two target areas: the first was the East End, especially the docks, and the second the City and West End. The attacks were ordered to begin on Saturday 7 September – but in the meantime, from the evening of Wednesday 4, Luftflotte 3 flew a number of hit-and-run raids across the Channel aimed at London's dockland, dropping what were obviously reconnaissance flares and a scattering of bombs. None was of great significance.

There was, though, something of much greater import discovered by an RAF reconnaissance flight patrolling the Channel that same Wednesday – something not only very interesting, but also decidedly unnerving. For what the plane had spotted and photographed was a group of approximately a hundred barges gathering on the coast near Flushing. The photographs required looking at twice, for until that

*". . . then, what's left over from the front room bedspread we could dye and make into cushion-covers for the parlour."*

day there had been no sign of any such activity along the coast. Hitler had been threatening invasion, of course; *everyone* knew that. Now was he finally planning to put his words into action?

Over the following days of that week reconnaissance planes spotted further concentrations of barges, some as large as 250 strong, assembling at ports such as Ostend, Dunkirk and Calais. The signs were now unmistakable: an invasion *was* imminent.

If further proof were needed, Fighter Command reported that Kesselring appeared to be massing his dive bombers along the French coast between Calais and Ghent, and there was a meteorological report that the Channel tides would be as favourable as at any time this year for a crossing during the weekend. To add the final touch to the rumours, four Germans were apprehended landing from a rowing boat on the south coast and admitted they were spies sent to report on troop movements in the area.

At 5.20 on the afternoon of Saturday 7 September, the British Chiefs of Staff met and came to the conclusion that an invasion seemed imminent and they must act. Plans for countering such an invasion – code-named 'Cromwell' – had been in readiness for some time, and though the Home Fleet was currently in Scapa Flow, the RAF and the Army were as prepared as they would ever be under the present circumstances.

If, of course, Hitler's original time schedule for invasion had gone as planned and not been thrown into disarray by the bravery of Dowding's pilots, then German forces would more than likely have stormed the south coast that weekend. As it was, Goering still had to 'exterminate British cities' before Hitler would order any such crossing.

None the less, the 'Cromwell' signal was sent out to the troops of Eastern and Southern Command. The Home Guard, too, were called out, some of the men summoned by the unauthorised ringing of church bells – the predetermined signal to be used only when paratroopers were actually *seen* landing – and for a time confusion reigned. Rumours, too, became rife – with stories of Germans landing here or being thrown back into the Channel somewhere else. Indeed, in the days that followed, such stories were common throughout much of the country, though the newspapers and radio maintained a diplomatic – and probably instructed – silence about 'the invasion that never was'. (Two accounts of these rumours and just how widely they spread are reprinted on page 168 in the panel 'The Day the Channel Caught Fire'.)

Whatever human error may have been responsible for signalling 'Cromwell' (and it may have been precipitated by the aerial bombardment of London which had just started), it none the less acted as a kind of warning for what certainly did take place on 7 September – the arrival of the first armada of German bombers hell-bent on laying waste one of the greatest cities in the world. How close they were to come to realising that objective forms the final phase of the story of the Battle of Britain.

*Two typical examples of English humour published while the Battle of Britain raged in the skies above the nation.* (above) *Russell Brockbank's idiosyncratic comment on 'Dog Fights',* Lilliput, *September 1940.* (left) *Tony Hickey's tribute to the imperturbable British housewife in* Punch, *28 August.*

*Although numbers of German airmen were rescued from the English Channel after their planes had crashed during the summer of 1940, none suffered the terrible fate claimed in the rumour of 'The Day the Channel Caught Fire'.*

## THE DAY THE CHANNEL CAUGHT FIRE

A protean rumour which has shown itself in various forms during this month has reached London in what may be its final and true shape. It began with a reported alarm in Cornwall, spreading to Hampshire, and heard by many: the Germans had landed somewhere in Dorset; in Kent; in Lincolnshire. This was officially denied.

Then a whisper started that the corpses of German soldiers, in full battle dress, had been washed up all round the coast. Presently the horrid detail that each corpse had its hands tied behind its back was added. I felt this was a sheer Quisling intended to foment indignation against the Royal Navy. Who else could have this notion or the opportunity of doing such a thing?

Then the tale grew into patent absurdity. The whole of the Channel from Weymouth to Devonport was covered with the corpses of stricken armies. We had apparently poured petrol all over the sea by a secret device and set fire to it and burnt the Germans all up.

The retailer of this piece of nonsense had pointed out to those who brought it to him that, if this were true, the entire population of the Reich must have perished, and also that no corpses drowned in the North Sea would get far beyond the Straits of Dover as the tide there would wash them to and fro.

After that the rumour died down, but today it has come back in a more plausible form. The Invasion had a dress rehearsal last week. The RAF attended it. The embarked *Wehr* did not like the prospect. The suspicion that this was no mere rehearsal produced a stampede.

The hospitals of Northern France are now filled with German soldiers, all shot in the back by the bullets of their commanding officers.

Naomi Royde Smith
*Time & Tide*, September 1940

# —11—

# 'THE WHOLE BLOODY WORLD'S ON FIRE!'

To most intents and purposes, the evening of Saturday 7 September began like any other in London. Despite all that had happened in the country during the previous weeks, the spirit of the capital as exemplified by the irrepressible Cockneys was as good as ever – and after a hard week, Saturday night was the night for a little fun, wasn't it? During the afternoon there had been several football matches in London at Chelsea, Millwall and West Ham as well as a greyhound meeting at New Cross, and most of the cinemas, theatres and pubs were either open or would be opening their doors shortly.

In the tight little streets of the Cockney stronghold of Silvertown, bounded on one side by the River Thames and on the other by the huge Royal Victoria Dock and Royal Albert Dock, men were returning home for their tea, eagerly looking forward to a few drinks and perhaps a game of darts or dominoes in one of the neighbourhood's cosy pubs. 'Old 'itler ain't goin' to get me and the missus dahn,' was a commonly expressed sentiment.

In the West End, those who had spent the day visiting the shops in Piccadilly and Oxford Street were thinking about taking trains home, while others who actually lived in the area were planning a night out to see a play or a film, with perhaps a meal beforehand. 'Of course, meals *nowadays* are nothing like they used to be before the war, my dear, but it's still nice to get away from it all for a

few hours,' might be heard in the vicinity of Knightsbridge.

In the City, most of the offices about Bank and Moorgate were quiet and deserted as would be expected at the weekend, though there were signs of activity near St Paul's where a few sightseers mingled with the members of the Civil Defence preparing for another night of watching the skies for enemy planes. 'Jerry's been over a few times recently, but those RAF chaps soon see him off,' remarked a Home Guard.

Though none of these Londoners knew it then, the night to come was to prove unlike anything they had ever experienced before.

As the capital prepared for tea-time, across the Channel Kesselring signalled his men to begin their new offensive. At a vantage point on the coast which was within sight of England, a special visitor had just arrived to witness what he hoped would be the decisive phase of the battle – Hermann Goering. Binoculars pressed to his eyes, the Reichsmarschall in his long white coat bedecked with medals watched as the first of 300 bombers and 600 short-range and long-range fighters climbed into the still bright sky. The time was just 4 p.m.

The attack on London was to be made in three separate waves at intervals of about twenty minutes, the whole operation scheduled to last for an hour before the planes turned for home. It was undoubtedly the strongest force that the commander of Luftflotte 2 could muster for what was the first major daylight raid on the capital. And once Kesselring had played his part, Sperrle was to follow up as soon as darkness fell with another force of 250 bombers.

*The devastation of London – this photograph taken by a* News Chronicle *photographer was banned from publication by the Censor.*

*'Pathetic groups of the homeless trudging along with bundles of what household possessions they had been able to salvage from their wrecked homes.' Another poignant photograph of the East End.*

The first groups of planes climbed laboriously from their bases to 15,000 feet where they assembled, en masse, for the crossing of the Channel. As they neared the English coast, a number of the Luftwaffe's fighters began to make diversionary attacks on coastal objectives and shipping off Kent and Essex. Fighter Command had, as always, received ample warning of the impending attack from the radar stations which had picked up the blips of the Germans gathering like some vast army of vultures. In all, 21 British squadrons were scrambled to do battle with the invaders.

Such, though, was the protection provided by the Messerschmitts for the bombers – combined with the fact that the English controllers understandably expected the Germans to be heading yet again for the vital air-fields, and had deployed their squadrons accordingly –

*(right) A direct hit on Silvertown. Eye-witness Mrs Joan Cook surveys the aftermath of the raids in a typical street in London's dockland.*

that the deadly armada reached its objective surprisingly unmolested and in full strength. The evening plans of the people of London were about to be devastatingly upset.

The first wave of bombers, Dornier 17s, had instructions to bomb the Royal Victoria Docks, while the aircraft behind were to hit the other shipping harbours including the East and West India Docks, as well as the oil installations along the Thames and the Royal Arsenal at Woolwich.

Joan Cook, who lived with her husband and five children on Albert Road, in Silvertown, never forgot the experience of the first German bombs plunging down on her neighbourhood. 'We were just having something to eat when we heard the sirens go,' she recalled. 'We'd heard them before, of course, so we got our things and went outdoors to go to the Anderson shelter. As soon as we were outside, there were these terrible bangs going off and everywhere seemed to be lit up. The explosions

semed to be coming from down the road near the docks. Then the pavement and houses began to shake and my husband shouted that we had better run to the shelter. Even before we were inside we could see flames leaping up into the sky.'

Later, Mrs Cook added: 'It was an experience far worse than the Silvertown explosion in the last war. The heat from the fires was terrific. But we didn't think about leaving the place – Albert Road was our home, wasn't it?'

It was the sound of the doors and windows of his rectory rattling, followed by the floor shaking, that first made the local priest, Father H.A. Wilson, aware of the bombs dropping on Silvertown. 'I didn't think I had a hope of living through that night,' he admitted later. 'I am not sure I even said a prayer, beyond the occasional "Oh, God!" – if that may be accounted a prayer. I was more frightened than I had ever been before.'

A Fleet Street journalist, David Pritchard, was just up

the road in Limehouse that night, near the West India Docks, when the German bombers struck. 'I was outside this public house with a group of friends when we heard the droning of planes overhead,' he said. 'Suddenly we heard a whirring, rushing sound. "That's a bomb!" a man behind me shouted. "Fall flat!" We all flung ourselves in the gutter in a sort of human chain. A few moments passed and the same man ordered us into the shelter.

'When the activity overhead died down, we came out again. What we had seen before was nothing to what we found then. The whole air was a bright blaze of gold. Just as we started to walk, we heard first a rushing, then a heavy explosion, and a brilliant firework display in the road directly in our path. A bomb had blocked the road. The magnesium flares and the flash of the explosion looked just like one of those old cinemas, with its rows and rows of electric lights in arches and cascades.'

With the reporter's instinct for news, David Pritchard busied himself collecting human interest stories for his paper – and one particular memory remained with him long after that first night of the Blitz. 'I remember talking to this woman who had driven a car over London Bridge that evening,' he recalled. 'She had come back to the East End over Tower Bridge. She said that nothing had moved her so much as the sight of the Tower of London. "It stood there squat and solid and contemptuous with the whole sky rosy behind it," she told me. "It symbolised the whole of our history. It will take a good deal more

(above) *'It's like the end of the world' – the famous photograph of St Paul's towering above a blitzed London.* (right) *A view from St Paul's towards the London docks after the German bombers had passed.*

than Hitler to shake us!"'

Another person who was actually *in* a famous London landmark, St Paul's, serving as a volunteer watcher, could only stare in silent horror as shower after shower of bombs rained down from the skies. Walter Harvey could never quite understand *how* the massive cathedral escaped being hit by the raiders – it seemed to him almost like divine intervention.

'We could see the planes going overhead,' Mr Harvey said, 'and all the time the explosions seemed to be getting closer to us. The drone of the bombers was deafening. None of us said a word, but we were all wondering how long it would be before a bomb hit us. I think I broke the silence first. "It's like the end of the world," I said. And one of the others replied, "It *is* the end of the world."'

It wasn't, of course, but for many people in the city that night it must have seemed like it. The writer A.P. Herbert, who was then serving as a petty officer in the Thames Auxiliary Patrol, witnessed the bombing from a boat ploughing up the Thames and wroter later: 'The Pool, below London Bridge, was a lake of light, and the

*The West End also felt the sting of the German bombers – but most residents, like Miss Hetty Singerman pictured here, still managed to smile through adversity.*

accumulated smoke and sparks of all the fires swept in a high wall across the river. When we got closer the scene was like a lake in Hell. Burning barges were drifting everywhere. We could hear the hiss and roar of conflagration, but we could not see it, so dense was the smoke.'

When Herbert finally reached one of the docks, he found 250 acres of timber on fire. 'There was a fire officer there trying to get the blaze under control. "See if you can get someone to send some more bloody pumps," he shouted to me. "The whole bloody world's on fire!"'

In stark contrast to this, another writer living in the West End remembered that Saturday evening for a display of typical British imperturbability. Speaking on BBC Radio on 10 September, Virginia Cowles said: 'I had an example of the stuff the women of Britain are made of on the Saturday night when the *blitzkrieg* on London started. The noise was very loud and the house shook several times, but both the maid and my secretary kept on with their normal routines. My secretary was so nervous that her hands trembled on the typewriter keys, but she insisted it was only a passing phase. "It takes a few minutes to become accustomed to the noise," she explained. "I'll be all right in a minute." And indeed she was. Ten minutes later she was calm and composed, her hands racing across the keys as though the noise outside were nothing more than the celebrations on Empire Day!'

Such enclaves of calm notwithstanding, in the skies above London Dowding's forces were being stretched to their limits. A Hurricane squadron leader who was assigned to tackle a cluster of raiders over the Docks said later: 'It was impossible to miss those we aimed at; there seemed oceans of them. At one time when we were immediately below one formation we pulled our noses up and sprayed them for all we were worth as they flew across the path of our fire.'

Not far away from these Hurricanes, a squadron of Spitfires actually managed to break up a group of enemy planes in the process of unloading their bombs over east London. Their squadron leader reported afterwards: 'We just gave them all we had got. Opening fire at nearly 150 yards range and breaking away when we could see the enemy cockpit completely filling our gunsight. That means we finished the attack at point-blank range. We went in practically in one straight line, all blazing away. I saw the Dornier I destroyed being hit in the engine and all along the starboard wing; all shapes and sizes of pieces flew off. Its engine burst into flames and the pilot turned away in a long dive towards the ground.'

There were also people down on the ground in a position to see what was happening. R.J. Cruickshank, a company director, was travelling into London on a train which slowed down as the bombers loomed overhead and then came to a complete standstill when the Fighter Command planes arrived on the scene.

'We all peered out of the window at what was going on,' he recalled. 'There was a man in the corner of my compartment who kept saying, "Those are our lads, bless 'em." It sounded silly when repeated a third time, yet the moment was heavy with the need for somebody to say *something*, and we were more grateful to him than we looked.

'The situation seemed to demand more than speech – a sort of combination of the gifts of the musician and the painter, to describe the rising flight of those Spitfires into the perilous blue. "Now," I thought, "it is the young men in those Spitfires who are saving London."'

Another eye-witness saw one of those brave young men give up his life in the defence of London. Arthur Smith, a stevedore on his way home to the East End, watched as two German fighters fired at a Spitfire pilot who had parachuted out of his machine.

'It was sheer cold-blooded murder,' he said the following day. 'The Spitfire was shot down in flames and the pilot baled out. As he floated down, two German fighters passed and re-passed him, pouring burst after burst of machine-gun fire into him. We could see the pilot sag in his harness, and then he fell on top of a barrage balloon. The crew hauled the balloon in and they got the pilot down. He was gravely wounded and I think he died on the way to hospital.'

A friend who was with Arthur Smith told reporters that he had been at a football match earlier in the afternoon and seen the German bombers appear shortly after the game had finished. One of the raiders was actually attacked over the ground by a British fighter, the man said, and there had been the biggest cheer of the afternoon from the dispersing 4000 spectators when it was seen to crash nearby!

As darkness fell over London, a large part of the East End and many buildings along the Thames were burning furiously despite the gallant efforts of the firemen, ARP workers and Home Guards. This undoubtedly made the task of the second wave of bombers from Sperrle's Luftflotte 3 that much easier when they arrived at 8.30 p.m. They, too, proceeded to release almost 300 hundred tons of high explosives and thousands of incendiary bombs into the inferno. This was virtually the same amount as had been unleashed by Kesselring's pilots – but targeted with

greater accuracy. When the last raider returned to France in the early hours of Sunday morning, the city had been under aerial seige for almost eight hours.

The cold light of dawn soon turned the confusion of smoke and flames into a stark picture of desolation. The roads and railways of London were at a standstill, buildings and homes by the thousand lay wrecked, and 430 people were dead and another 1600 seriously injured. Fighter Command estimated that the Germans had lost a total of 41 bombers in the raid, but the cost to Dowding's men had been high, too: 28 fighters destroyed or badly damaged and 17 pilots killed or seriously wounded.

The worst-hit area of all in London was Silvertown, which had actually been cut off by fire for part of the night and those residents requiring urgent hospital attention had had to be rescued by boat. Winston Churchill was just one of those who visited the community on Sunday morning during a tour of inspection of the battered city. Of the Prime Minister's visit to Silvertown, historian Angus Calder wrote: 'The Prime Minister passed down roads covered with debris and broken glass and great coils of firehose. At one point, tallow from a burnt candle factory made the road slippery; at another, the air was thick with odours from a scent factory. Elsewhere, there was the choking smell of burning wood. Red-eyed, weary, filthy firemen were still struggling with the many fires which yet raged.'

During his tour, Churchill passed pitiful groups clutching what belongings they still possessed, but – says Calder – when they saw him they dropped what they were carrying and cheered. 'Putting his hat on the end of his stick, he twirled it round and roared, "Are we downhearted?" and they shouted back, "No!" with astonishing gusto.'

Newspapermen from the national press were also soon on the scene, a reporter from the *Daily Mail* informing his readers: 'The Germans failed on Saturday to perpetrate a second Rotterdam in London because of the dogged courage of those manning our defences, the services and the civilians.'

A writer for the *Daily Telegraph* painted a rather more personal picture of what he saw.

'After a sleepless night, while their Anderson shelters rocked with the explosion of bombs and the crash of guns, the people of East London carried on today with their usual amazing spirit,' he wrote. 'Several hundred began the search for new homes as soon as the "all clear" sounded. Whole streets had been destroyed and many other houses demolished. But people gathered their possessions together and piled them into perambulators. With children in their arms, they started their walk to friends and relatives.

'The morale of the people was astonishing. As they

## HEROES WITH DIRTY FACES

They called us 'The Heroes with Dirty Faces' – the 25,000 men and women of the Auxiliary Fire Service who were at the centre of London's Civil Defence system battling against the Blitz and bombs. Our casualties were high – higher, at one time, than the armed services' – but nothing was going to stop us from helping the men and women of the city.

During the Blitz the usual procedure was to order crews like us from the outskirts into central London. We would often be out on a job for 24 hours or even longer, frequently getting bombed, occasionally machine gunned.

We were inevitably hungry, too, our one and only uniform soaking wet. We would return to our stations so exhausted we would flop down on our straw mattresses just as we were.

Sometimes we had to remain out on the streets for a couple of weeks, with no accommodation, no food, nothing. We had to depend on the good nature of the public to feed and water us!

At first, in 1939, we used to say the AFS stood for 'Always Filling Sandbags' – but then came the Blitz. I knew fear all right, but the most fearful part was coming home and hoping your house was still standing and your wife and family were all right.

I remember people coming up to us, sobbing, crying, asking us to put their fire out. But you couldn't. You had to go on to bigger ones. This was tragic and heartbreaking at times.

There was an old lady who emerged from a badly damaged house after a nasty raid with a steaming pot of tea for the boys.

'Excuse the pot,' she said, 'but it's quite clean. I didn't have a jug that was big enough.'

The pot was a *chamber pot* – but the tea still tasted good!

For me the war was terrible, dreadful, but in a sort of way rewarding. Everyone was very friendly and helpful. There didn't seem to be any class barriers. There was a great *camaraderie*.

It was an enriching experience, but for the wrong reasons. It is a pity we couldn't have had those experiences without the horror of the holocaust.

Leslie Broughton
*Daily Express*, 3 September 1979

were walking to their new homes many were laughing and joking among themselves. Some families took care of children whose parents were dead or injured, and made long journeys across London to escort them to the homes of relatives. Women went on preparing the Sunday dinner, even though they had no water or gas. They borrowed water from more fortunate neighbours and lit fires to roast the joint.

'In a dockland tavern, where every window had been blown out by a bomb which fell across the road, they were collecting for the Spitfire Fund! The licensee of a hotel gave up his saloon bar for housing people whose houses were no longer tenable.

'In several streets neighbours were making a whip-round for those who had lost their belongings. The morale of the people was summed up in the words of one Mayor who said, "They have taken it on the chin."'

A *Daily Sketch* reporter touring the same streets painted an equally heart-warming picture.

'All round, small houses and here and there a school lay shattered,' he wrote, 'but East London was not cowering. Sunday is a favourite marriage day that way and over roads littered with debris rolled motorcars bedecked with white. Weddings were not being put off for this. Side by side with these festivals were to be seen pathetic groups of the homeless trudging along with bundles of what household possessions they had been able to salvage from wrecked homes.

'A trolley bus stood leaning over with its sides riddled with holes from bomb splinters, all the glass gone, the heavy tyres deflated, and part of one side had been ripped off by the blast. It stood there deserted amidst a sea of shattered small houses.

'No one who saw that blaze with the thick smoke overhanging the bright flames will ever forget it. But for the prompt and efficient work by the firemen of the capital and the many volunteers, the blaze and the material damage done by it would have been far worse.' (An account by a member of the Auxiliary Fire Service of his experiences is given in the panel 'Heroes with Dirty Faces'.)

London and its people had barely time to draw breath and patch up the worst damage before Kesselring despatched another 200 bombers on Monday 9 September – just as weary workers everywhere were sitting down to their tea. This time, however, Fighter Command was prepared for an attack on the capital and after some fierce scrapping over Kent and Essex was able to turn back the first wave of 100 bombers before they reached London. With orders not to return loaded, many of the German pilots jettisoned their bombs on and around the unfortunate city of Canterbury.

The second wave was also strongly resisted. How-

Members of the ground staff at Millwall FC clearing up the debris after a bomb had struck the terracing at The Den.

ever, the pilots of the bombers that *did* get through were understandably nervous, and with little thought for accuracy indiscriminately bombed places as far apart as Richmond to the west of London and Camberwell to the east. The cost of this day's raids was 28 German machines to Fighter Command's 19 – a significant improvement over Saturday and undoubtedly a tactical victory for Dowding. The cost in lives lost in London was 370.

For Goering's Luftwaffe, after the euphoria of the raids on Saturday, this was a real setback. Once again,

it seemed, they had introduced a new strategy of attack – and just as quickly it had been countered by the British, in particular their amazingly resilient and still remarkably numerous fighter pilots. On 10 September Hitler decided to postpone once again his decision about invasion. He would now wait until the 14th – with the crossing to be made as previously established ten days later on the 24th, *if* everything was favourable.

During the next seven days the fate of the nation hung in the balance. The 'Spitfire Summer' was about to reach its climax.

*Members of the rescue teams drag the body of a badly injured woman from the ruins of her bomb-damaged London home.*

# ONE FATEFUL NIGHT

My home is situated in the centre of a triangle formed by Woolwich Arsenal, North Weald Fighter Aerodrome and the Enfield Small Arms Factory – all frequent targets of the German bombers whose raids on London were taking place day and night. I was fortunate in being at home throughout the entire 'Battle of London'. My ship was commissioning at Tilbury, about 30 miles away, and I was able to get home each evening.

I shall always owe a debt of gratitude to Fate that I was able to be at home during this period. The daily and nightly visits of the Nazis who fondly believed they were smashing London into subjection left me, as they left most Londoners, singularly undisturbed. One's nerves were undoubtedly a little strained, and in most cases the prospect of a peaceful sleep after the day's work was little more than a fond dream. But London certainly *did* carry on.

My wife, Rena, as conductress of a Green Line coach, did her job bravely and well – but no better, nor more bravely than did thousands of other women who were filling men's jobs. I was unworried because I was near my wife. I felt that because of that she would be safe – nothing could possibly happen to *us*. (What egotistical creatures men are!) Or if it did, we would at least be together. . . .

Rena and I were sitting by the fire about 9 o'clock one evening. The sirens sounded, but apart from a glance at the blackout we took no notice. We talked and listened to the wireless. My dog, Flip, scratched and whined at the kitchen door as he always does when the sirens go. We let him in and he took up his favourite position on the hearthrug.

Soon the bombs began to fall in the distance. The regular evening symphony of those days had once more commenced. We hardly interrupted our talking, although Flip jumped onto my lap and snuggled up close. The heavy guns in the field opposite our house opened up. Boom! Boom! All the windows and doors shook. Flip trembled and looked at me; wondering perhaps at the murderous folly of men. But he too was well used to this kind of entertainment. He too felt safe while he was near to those he loved.

Suddenly the roar of planes was heard approaching and a terrific crash sounded uncomfortably near. Then another, and another, each louder than the one before. Rena flung herself into my arms and Flip whined and crawled under the armchair.

Then, CRASH! The house shook violently – the lights went out – there was a noise of glass and wood shattering, and the plaster from the roof fell on to us. We flung ourselves on the floor in the corner. Rena was shaking and crying – she clung to me. I did my best to calm her, but I, too, was far from calm. Anger – a mad, blind, hateful anger seized me. My God, how I hated Hitler, the Nazis, Germans. Had I had the power to destroy every one of them in that moment I would have used that power ruthlessly!

A few seconds – minutes – hours – I don't know how long – we clung together. The planes passed – the din died down – I could hear screaming as we made our way outside. Roof, doors and windows were gone from my house, but we were alive and uninjured. The next street was completely destroyed – already nothing remained but a few walls and piles of bricks and mortar which hid mutilated human bodies. The bodies of wives, mothers, children, sweethearts. Such is total war, and such, thank God, was the spirit of the people of London in those dark months that London still lives – and in the midst of the scars that remain her people can still say with pride that 'London can take it!'

Lieutenant J.M. Moran, RNR
*Daily Sketch*, 9 October 1940

# —12—

# THE END OF SUMMER – THE DAWN OF VICTORY

The week of Monday 9 September to Sunday 15 September has gone down in British history with typical understatement as the time 'London Met the Challenge'. It was in reality the week when the Nazi threat, poised on the nation's very doorstep, was stemmed and, as a result, turned irreversibly back in the direction from which it had come.

Today, fifty years later, it is almost impossible to put into words the mixture of courage, determination, pride and sheer guts that the people of London showed in the face of almost unrelenting attacks by German bombers. And by so doing they provided the inspiration for everyone – both those throughout the rest of the nation and the uncommitted abroad – which would eventually sweep the forces of the free world on to their great victory against the Axis powers.

Winston Churchill knew precisely what was at stake at this time, and he saw it in the same terms as Drake's confrontation with the Spanish Armada, or Nelson standing between the country and Napoleon's great army at Boulogne. Speaking in Parliament that week, he said: 'These cruel, wanton, indiscriminate bombings are, of course, a part of Hitler's invasion plans. He hopes, by killing large numbers of civilians, and women and children, that he will terrorise and cow the people of this mighty imperial city, and make them a burden and an anxiety to the Government and thus distract our attention unduly from the ferocious onslaught he is preparing. Little does he know the spirit of the British nation, or the tough fibre of the Londoners, whose forebears played a leading part in the establishment of Parliamentary institutions and who have been bred to value freedom above their lives.'

Even those who might have found it difficult to think about any long-term significance as far as the days they were living through were concerned could not deny Churchill's argument, or the feeling that *if* they gave in, Hitler was just a wing and a prayer away from invasion and, in all probability, conquest. Daily life, though, had to go on, and one Londoner, Ivor Halstead, working in the city during those tense days, noted his impressions in his diary which he wrote – as he recalled – 'while hostile planes droned overhead'.

'With battles raging above them day and night, Londoners do a lot of grumbling and sometimes tired nerves make for irritation, but there is no fear and no panic. Cockney humour survives. It is as inextinguishable as Cockney courage.

'A partly demolished tavern I passed has the notice up: 'Open as Usual'. The little coffee-shop next door, full also of *blitzkrieg* apertures, has improved on it and announces blithely: 'More Open Than Usual'. A shattered refreshment shop has the sign: 'Never mind Goering. Come in through the nearest hole. We still have command of the teas!'

'"One thing Hitler has done for us," said an old woman in the tube lift who had lost her home the night before, "he's knocked off the rent days!" I heard a workman say, "I've lost all the furniture, but blimey, thank God I've got me legs left." There was a raid when a young

*With a mixture of great courage and skill, Fighter Command drove the Luftwaffe from the skies of Britain in the early weeks of September 1940.*

*Life goes on in Birmingham – just as it did elsewhere in the nation – as the Battle of Britain drew to a close.*

girl started to powder and make up her face in the tram. The conductor watched her for a time, and then said, "Any gent 'ere like to borrow my shaving tackle?"

'"This war's hittin' pluto-democrats like me, 'Arry," said another workman, showing his tiny wage-packet to a bus driver. "'Ere's my weekly pittance cut dahn again." Came the swift, and in my opinion brilliant, retort from the driver: "When yer gets home, Bert, you'll 'ave ter sit dahn with the trouble and strife at the old Joanna and sing, 'Mock of wiges cleft for me'."'

Frederick Salfield of the *Daily Telegraph* was also abroad that week in the very heart of London – Lambeth – and talked to a typical housewife, Maud Smithers, about how she and her neighbourhood were getting along under the ordeal of German bombs.

'"It was a bit 'ot at the time," she admitted, referring to a particular bomb that had demolished a house five doors away. "But you know 'ow it is – in the morning, with the sun shining and the children playing in the streets as usual, it all seems quite different."

'"I tell you, mister – and I'm not just kidding you because you're a newspaper chap – the people round 'ere is A1, and no mistake. Not a bleedin' moan out of one of 'em. There was one chap – very badly 'urt 'e was – and all 'e wanted to know was if 'is wife was OK. And there was the old lady at No. 51 – the 'ouse came down on 'er and they dragged 'er out of the basement and sent 'er to 'ospital. She didn't want to go. Would 'ave it she was quite all right. Not bloody bad for over seventy!"'

Tom Oliver also observed workaday London at this time, and he wrote in an article for the *Evening News*: 'Every morning, no matter how many bombs have been dropped in the night, London's transport runs, letters are delivered, milk and bread comes to the door, confectioners get their supplies, and the fruiterers' windows are filled. To achieve this marvel thousands of men and women have to work and travel through the black-out and the Blitz.

'Hitler's envoys were roaring over London for five of the ten hours I passed studying the conditions at a railway terminus, the GPO sorting office at Mount Pleasant, a factory on the outskirts, a large bakery, a fire station, a bus depot and a Tube station. At none of these places did work cease for a single second. The German bombers may prick like autumn wasps, they may hinder, but they will never destroy the vast mechanism serving and feeding 8,000,000 people.'

Those living in the capital at this time also recall with great admiration the 150,000 Civil Defence workers – the men and women in steel helmets with grubby faces whose acts of bravery rescuing bomb victims, putting out fires, helping to repair gas and water mains and telegraph wires as well as generally marshalling the public, helped London get through the nightmare of *blitzkrieg*. Many

*A contemporary portrait of Douglas Bader – and the first newspaper story about his amazing achievements.* Daily Telegraph, *16 September.*

# IDENTITY OF LEGLESS PILOT

◆

## LEADS CANADIAN SQUADRON

### By MAJOR C. C. TURNER

I learn that the Hurricane pilot who, although he lost both legs in a pre-war crash, shot down a Dornier 17 in a week-end raid was Flying Officer D. R. S. Bader.

He is the 30-year-old son of Mrs. Hobbs, wife of the Rector of Sprotborough, near Doncaster. He performed daring aerobatics in the R.A.F. display at Hendon in 1931. He played Rugby for the R.A.F., the Combined Services and Harlequins, and was so good a scrum-half that he would in all probability have got his England cap. He also played cricket and squash.

In December, 1931, he lost control when flying over his aerodrome and crashed heavily. After the loss of both legs, he was invalided out of the service, but he became so skilful in the use of his metal legs that he could still He became the representative of an oil combine, and had the pedals of his car altered so that he could drive. He eve learned to play golf.

### POSTED TO FIGHTERS

Within nine months he was in the air again, a fully qualified civil pilot. When war broke out, in the words of a friend, " he almost went down on his hands and knees to the Air Ministry to take him back into the R.A.F." He passed a test with flying colours and was posted to a fighter squadron.

A few months ago he was taking off when his engine failed and he had a minor crash. Both his metal legs were badly bent, but an artificer straightened them and half an hour later he was up in the air again. Now he is leading a squadron of Canadians.

were injured; others gave their lives helping their fellow men. According to official figures, during the course of the war 1206 members of the Home Guard and 624 in the home front war auxiliary services fell as casualties.

On Wednesday 11 September, Luftflotte 2 and 3 combined to carry out the third major raid on London. Shortly after lunch, Kesselring attacked with a force of 100 bombers – much smaller than on previous occasions – but virtually all the pilots managed to reach the City and the docks and damage them extensively. Among the locations to be hit was Buckingham Palace, though neither the King or Queen, nor members of the royal family were hurt. Almost immediately afterwards, Sperrle's pilots attacked the city, again with considerable success. The cost this day to the Luftwaffe was 24 aircraft, and to Fighter Command 29.

Hitler was understandably pleased when he heard how this new offensive was going, believing the British losses to be much higher than they actually were, and expressed his satisfaction to the Luftwaffe. The achievements of Goering and his pilots were 'above all praise', he said, and he told a group of generals at lunch that he was now beginning to feel Britain could well be defeated by air attacks *alone*. Therefore, he saw little point in ordering an invasion which would be difficult and undoubtedly highly costly in terms of men and weapons. Interestingly, these remarks were not made in public, where the Fuehrer continued to state that he believed an invasion was the *only* way of subduing the British – although he did stipulate that a prerequisite to this remained superiority in the air.

The consequence of this obvious inner turmoil was that Hitler put off making a decision about the invasion yet again – to the 17th, which would thus mean a crossing ten days later on the 27th. From the German point of view, this would be a make-or-break day, for 27 September was the last date before 8 October when it was known there would be a favourable tide. Once the timing went beyond that, there was a very real danger that the unpredictable British winter would arrive and make a nonsense of all the carefully organised plans.

In London, Winston Churchill was aware how close his enemy was to unleashing his invasion forces and on 11 September went on the radio to explain his hopes and fears in a typically forthright manner to the listening audience of millions. It was another stirring oration by the master of words, which undoubtedly raised hearts and minds throughout the nation. The main text of the Prime Minister's speech, 'A Very Important Day in Our History', which so stirringly captures the atmosphere in that September week, is reprinted on page 205.

On Friday and Saturday the Luftwaffe again crossed the Channel, with bombers and fighters making a bee-

*September 15, 'Battle of Britain Day'. A Spitfire attacks a Heinkel 111 over London – a reconstruction of the drama in the air for the famous 1969 movie The Battle of Britain.*

line for London. On these occasions, Fighter Command lost about twenty aircraft each day – much the same as their enemy – but it was the rather desultory way in which the British pilots parried these thrusts that added further conviction to the German belief that the RAF must be on its last legs.

The explanation was actually more prosaic than this. From 11 September the Germans had instituted a programme of 'jamming' radio waves, which also interfered with the radar system, and though not wholly successful had still made it difficult for Dowding's pilots to locate the raiders and get themselves into their normally strong position to attack. But, preferring to believe that the long-awaited moment when the British were on their knees had arrived, Kesselring – after consultation with Goering – decided to throw the whole weight of his forces, over 100 bombers and a little under 400 fighters, into two major daylight raids on London on 15 September. Perhaps if he had studied the omens and realised he had picked a Sunday, the

same day of the week that had seen one of the great decisive British victories of history – namely Waterloo – he might have had second thoughts . . .

As it transpired, that memorable Sunday in 1940 that we still remember with gratitude each year as 'Battle of Britain Day' was warm with clear skies – 'one of those autumn days when the countryside looks at its best', to quote the usually unemotional Dowding. Perhaps, like many others, he was only to remember it so clearly afterwards because of the page of history he and his pilots wrote that day with their courage and, in some cases, their lives.

It was due to the good visibility on that Sunday that a large number of people in the south of England were able to watch from the ground what one writer called the 'Luftwaffe's humiliation'. Just after 11.30 a.m. the first waves of Kesselring's bombers appeared in the distance over the south coast.

By a curious coincidence, Winston Churchill had slipped out of Chequers that morning with his wife and stopped in at Air Vice-Marshal Park's headquarters in

*'Bombers' Prey' – a poignant photograph by Cecil Beaton which helped to boost the morale of Londoners when it was published in September 1940.*

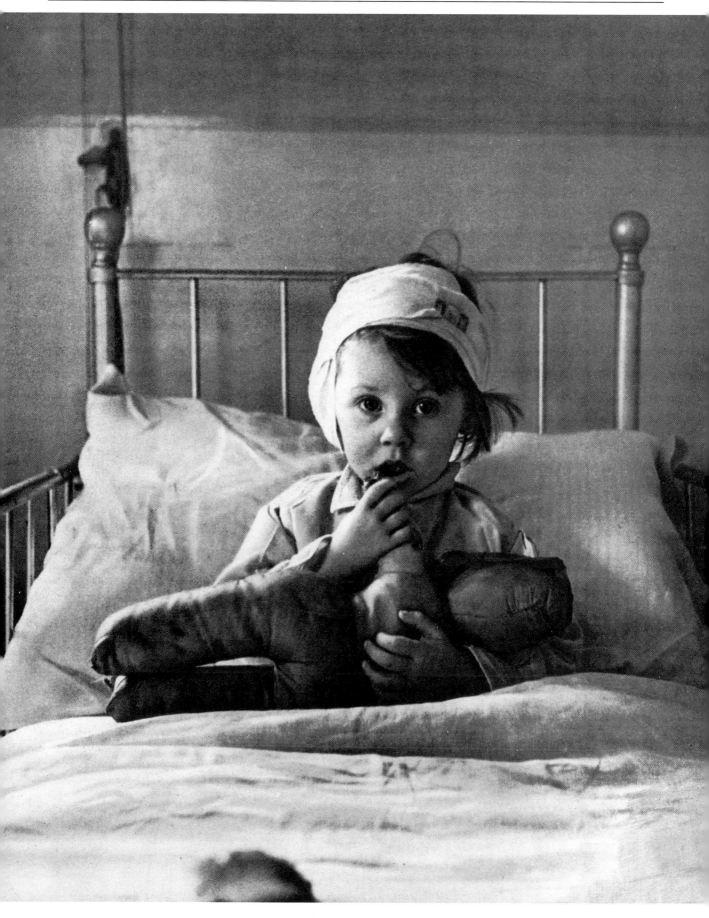

*Despite the damage caused to all forms of transport in London, life continued in the city and vital supplies of food never ceased to get through.* (above) *A photograph of wrecked vehicles in Blackfriars Road, and* (overleaf) *St Pancras Station after a raid.*

Uxbridge. The Prime Minister was therefore able to watch the drama he had predicted being recreated with model aircraft on a map in the busy operations room. When it became evident from the huge numbers of models being placed on the map that the Germans had gathered a mighty force, Churchill and Park and the other Fighter Command personnel in the room might have been forgiven for wondering if here, finally, was the preamble to invasion. Legend has it that during the hours that followed, the Prime Minister was so engrossed that for once the large cigar in his mouth remained unlit.

The pilots of Park's No. 11 Group had no time for thoughts of invasion as they were scrambled for action to meet the invaders. One anonymous Spitfire squadron leader in the Group, who was among the first to face the Germans on this aupicious day, later described his impressions for the press.

'The 15th of September dawned bright and clear at Croydon,' he said. 'It never seemed to do anything else during those exciting weeks of August and September. But to us it was just another day. We weren't interested in Hitler's entry into London; most of us were wondering whether we would have time to finish breakfast before the final blitz started. We were lucky.

'It was about mid morning that the sirens started wailing and the order came through to rendezvous at 20,000 feet. As we were climbing in a southerly direction at 15,000 feet we saw 30 Heinkels supported by 50 ME 109s about 4000 feet above them, and 20 ME 109s in a flank approaching us from above. We turned and climbed, flying in the same direction as the bombers with the whole squadron strung out in echelon to port up-sun, so that each man had a view of the enemy.

'"A" flight timed their attack to perfection,' the squadron leader continued, 'coming down-sun in a power dive on the enemy's left flank. As each pilot was selecting his own man, the ME 110 escort roared in to intercept with cannons blazing at 1000 yards range, but they were two seconds too late – too late to engage our fighters, but just in time to make them hesitate long enough to miss the bomber leader. Two Heinkels heeled out of the formation.

'Meanwhile the ME 110s had flashed out of sight, leaving the way clear for "B" flight, as long as the ME 109s stayed above. "B" flight leader knew how to bide his time, but just as he was about to launch his attack the Heinkels did the unbelievable thing. They turned south; into the sun; and into him. With his first burst the leader destroyed the leading bomber which blew up with such force that it knocked a wing off the left-hand bomber. A little bank and burst from his guns sent the right-hand Heinkel out of the formation with smoke pouring out of both engines. Before returning

home, the leader knocked down an ME 109. Four aircraft destroyed for an expenditure of 1200 rounds was the best justification for our new tactics.'

With those opening shots Fighter Command had set the pattern for the day. Whatever success the Germans might have enjoyed in the previous days of that week were to count as nothing as Park's men blasted enemy bombers and fighters out of the sky. From the underground headquarters in Uxbridge, the call went out for Groups No. 10 and 12 to stand by to join the fray. And when the pilots from Leigh-Mallory's Group joined the action, turning the skies over southern England into a vast cobweb of white vapour trails that thousands watched, fascinated, from below, it was already becoming clear that the bombers were beginning to falter in their drive for London and the fighter escort was similarly growing increasingly worried about the disruption among its charges.

For Squadron Leader James McComb of No. 611 Squadron based at Digby – one of Leigh-Mallory's Group – it was to be the day when he and his men went from being substitutes in the wings to members of the attacking first team. For several weeks they had been held in reserve, listening from their base in the Midlands while the Germans attacked London and the south.

'As those summer days went by we began to despair,' the Squadron Leader recalled afterwards in a BBC radio broadcast, 'feeling that we were to be left out of the show. Then at last our chance came on the morning of September 15. Operations rang – "Squadron to go to F. at once." Then at our station for the first time, over the loud-speaker: "Squadrons scramble London 20,000 feet."

'It came so quickly. One instant I was asleep on the grass by my aeroplane; a short moment while fumbling fingers strapped me in my Spitfire – my inside felt cold and seemed to be turning over – then bumping across the aerodrome in formation. I do not know what happened after that until a queer artificial voice came over the radio: "Two hundred bandits crossing Dover flying north at 20,000 feet; some more very high up." The sky was empty, and everything below us seemed still, as if the world was asleep.

'Then suddenly we saw them, a huge great rectangle of black bombers, ack-ack bursting all around them, and we were diving towards them. I remember a Heinkel flying across my nose so close that I saw the pilot looking at me. There were aircraft all around – bombers falling out of formation, black dots of fighters climbing and diving. Away on the left a long black trail of smoke and a blazing dot going straight down.

'Then it was all over, and I was back at the aerodrome. Excited pilots recounting their experi-

ences. I only realised then that I had fired my guns. I felt it had been a good day – little did I know that twice more that day I would climb up over London, fight, and come home again.'

While these scraps had been going on in the sky, London had been showered as much by the debris of falling German planes as by bombs. A Dornier had crashed just outside Victoria Station and its crew had parachuted down into Kennington Oval. A Messerschmitt with its pilot still strapped into his seat had plunged into the Thames near Westminster Bridge, which was lined with crowds watching the battle. Elsewhere, flaming German machines had fallen on to the city or the suburbs to the accompaniment of cheering.

By 12.30 the battle was over and the German force, much depleted, had scuttled for France. Across England, people settled down to their Sunday lunch and, half an hour later, turned on their radios for the *One O'Clock News*, read by Frank Phillips in his always reassuring tones. Though the news contained no details of casualties, it informed the hushed listeners that anti-aircraft guns had achieved considerable success against the raiders, and that at least fifty British fighters had been engaged in battles over the city.

The traditional British Sunday lunch remained undisturbed for almost an hour and a half before Kesselring returned to the fray with two more waves of bombers, one consisting of 150 aircraft and the other 100. As a diversion, Sperrle flew a small number of unescorted bombers to attack Portland, though they did very little damage. Twenty-one Fighter Command squadrons were despatched to meet the two large groups, and the skies from the Thames Estuary to Dover became the scene of furious dog-fights. It was soon evident, however, that the RAF was more than the equal of the Luftwaffe.

The stories of the pilots who flew on this day are many and have been told countless times in individual memoirs and histories of the Battle of Britain. They talk of death-defying aerial manoeuvres and battles, and of men showing such skill and bravery that no German pilot who returned home would ever again believe that the British could be beaten over their own air space. The legends speak, too, of the 60 fighters from No. 12 Group, the British, Canadian, Polish and

*The German bombs fell indiscriminately on London.* (left) *The King and Queen inspect the damage caused to Buckingham Palace on 10 September; while* (overleaf) *a group of East End children, many of whom have lost their homes, pose for a photographer on the same day.*

*Another of Bryan de Grineau's powerful on-the-spot sketches, this one of the Civil Defence Services at work in the area of the Rotherhithe Docks after a German air raid on Wednesday 11 September.*

Czech fighters (among whom was the famous 'Ace of Aces', the legless warrior Squadron Leader Douglas Bader) who constituted the most formidable fighter formation the Luftwaffe had ever seen, and who engaged the enemy in the most destructive and perhaps greatest single engagement of the entire battle. To the bomber crews pursued by these aces it was, quite simply, a day of terror, for which those who survived thanked their lucky stars.

For me, no account better symbolises the spirit that ensured victory that day than the story of Group Captain S.F. Vincent, commander of the Northolt sector of Group 11. Flying in a lone Hurricane to see how his men were faring over London, this RAF veteran suddenly saw coming towards him a large formation of German bombers and fighters.

'There were no other British fighters in sight,' Group Captain Vincent said afterwards with a laconic smile, 'so I made a head-on attack on the first section of the bombers, opening at 600 yards and closing to 200 yards. They seemed totally bemused by the fact I was on my own, and several of the leading bombers fell out of the formation and turned away.

'I made further attacks on the retreating bombers, each attack from climbing beam on. Another Dornier left the formation and lost height. With no ammunition left I could not finish it off. I last saw the bomber at 3000 feet dropping slowly.'

The Group Captain's last words might almost have been a prediction of the Luftwaffe's fortunes from this moment on. For Kesselring's armada had been decisively beaten by Fighter Command. A tally at the end of the second raid showed that the Germans had lost 60 aircraft to Fighter Command's 26. (An over-enthusiastic RAF bulletin that night actually put the figure at 183 German planes lost to the RAF's 28, with 14 pilots safe!)

*The Times* on Monday morning again carried another front-page banner, declaring: 'Britain Strikes Back!' In fact, as history has shown, the nation, and in particular its fighter pilots, had done much, *much* more than that.

According to most historians of the period, the Battle of Britain as a contest waged in the skies over England effectively ended on that evening of 15 September. For a while Goering still believed that further heavy air attacks would bring about the downfall of Dowding and his men – though he could no longer argue as to the paucity of their numbers – but the Luftwaffe simply did not have enough aircraft available for such massive raids. The ranks of the bomber crews had also been severely depleted, not to say demoralised. The Reichsmarschall's dream of air superiority paving the way to an invasion of Britain was now just that –

merely a dream!

For the people of Britain there were still dark days ahead, but there was more than a glimmer of hope on the horizon. They could smile, too, at the bombastic claims still being broadcast from Germany, and even laugh outright at one absurd report by Bremen Radio on 16 September that Goering himself had just flown over London in a bomber to see for himself the terrible damage his men had inflicted. The story was patently false, as the German leader was simply too fat to get through the narrow door of a Dornier!

On 17 September Hitler announced that he was postponing the invasion of Britain 'until further notice' – a decision some historians believe he had already made after hearing the accounts of the battle on that fateful Sunday when it was made perfectly evident that Fighter Command was 'far from defeated'. The next day, following a series of bold strikes by Bomber Command over the Channel to attack the clusters of barges dotted along the French coast – and the sinking of 84 of them – the Fuehrer ordered that the invasion fleet was to be disbanded forthwith.

Though German bombing operations against London and other cities continued throughout the winter and into 1941 – with varying degrees of success – and the German High Command did once more review its plans for invasion the following spring, by 31 October (according to the Ministry of Defence's reckoning) the Battle for Britain was at an end. It seemed a most appropriate day – for it also marked the festival of Hallowe'en. The spectre of Nazi evil would not, after all, darken any British doorstep.

It merely remained for the indomitable Winston Churchill to have the last words on this great British triumph. And in his history of the war written some years later, this is how he put it.

'Although post-war information has shown that the enemy's losses on September 15 were only 56, this day was the crux of the Battle of Britain. That night our Bomber Command attacked in strength the shipping in the ports from Boulogne to Antwerp. At Antwerp particularly heavy losses were inflicted. On September 17, as we now know, the Fuehrer decided to postpone invasion indefinitely. It was not until October 12 that the invasion was formally called off till the following spring. In July 1941 it was postponed again by Hitler till the spring of 1942, "by which time the Russian campaign will be completed". This was a vain but an important imagining. On February 13, 1942, Admiral Raeder had his final interview on the invasion and got Hitler to agree to a complete "stand down". Thus perished the German's great plan of conquest. And September 15, 1940 may stand as the date of its demise.'

## THE STORY OF ENERGETIC ERNIE

### Recounted by Anthony Gordon

The gallant and dangerous work of London's rescue squads is not without its humours, as I have seen for myself in my own squad. Take the example of one of the members whom we call 'Energetic Ernie'.

Ernie is alive – but only just. He's usually to be seen creeping around like a man whose last trouser button has just come off, and neither bombs nor shrapnel nor tottery buildings can shift him out of his steady gait.

I remember he was with me on the first night of the *blitzkrieg*. We were rushed to a bombed block of flats. Up on the second floor was an old gentleman and Ernie helped him through the window and on to the ladder. They made a good pair.

Slowly, so slowly, they came down the ladder. It seemed like an eternity before they were both safely on the ground. I spoke to the old man, expecting to hear a few words of gratitude. Instead, all I got was: 'My good man, would you mind going back and getting my false teeth off the wash-stand?'

One day last week we saw Ernie move fast, really fast. He had to go down into the basement of a bombed house to find some insurance policies. I watched him slowly squeeze through the rubbish and, torch in hand, disappear below.

Ten seconds later, Energetic Ernie came out of that hole like an express train. 'Run! Quick!' he shouted.

'What is it,' I asked, 'a time bomb?'

'No,' he yelled, 'the biggest blinking rat I've ever seen in my life!'

BBC Radio broadcast
24 September 1940

*A rescue squad saves yet another victim of German bombs.*

Winston Churchill,
who led the nation to victory in
the Battle of Britain, on a tour of inspection in the
streets of London.

# A VERY IMPORTANT DAY IN OUR HISTORY

### Speech by Winston Churchill, 11 September 1940

A great air battle is being fought out between our fighters and the German Air Force. Whenever the weather is favourable, waves of German bombers, protected by fighters, often three or four hundred at a time, surge over this island, especially the promontory of Kent, in the hope of attacking military and other objectives by daylight. However, they are met by our fighter squadrons and nearly always broken up; and their losses average three to one in machines and six to one in pilots. This effort of the Germans to secure daylight mastery of the air over England is, of course, the crux of the whole war. So far it has failed conspicuously. It has cost them very dear.

On the other hand, for Germany to invade this country without having secured mastery of the air would be a very hazardous undertaking. Nevertheless, all their preparations for invasion on a great scale are steadily going forward. Several hundreds of self-propelled barges are moving down the coasts of Europe, from the German and Dutch harbours to the ports of northern France. Besides this, convoys of merchant ships in tens of dozens are being moved through the Straits of Dover into the Channel, dodging along from port to port under the protection of the new batteries which the Germans have built on the French shore. Behind these clusters of ships and barges there stand very large numbers of German troops, awaiting the order to go on board and set out on their very dangerous and uncertain voyage across the sea.

We cannot tell when they will try to come; we cannot be sure that in fact they will try at all; but no one should blind himself to the fact that a heavy, full-scale invasion of this island is being prepared with all the usual German thoroughness and method, and that it may be launched now – upon England, upon Scotland, or upon Ireland, or upon all three. If this invasion is going to be tried at all, it does not seem that it can be long delayed. The weather may break at any time.

Every man and woman will therefore prepare himself to do his duty, whatever it may be, with special pride and care. Our fleets and flotillas are very powerful and numerous; our Air Force is at the highest strength it has ever reached – and it is conscious of its proved superiority, not indeed in numbers, but in men and machines. Our shores are well fortified and strongly manned, and behind them, ready to attack the invaders, we have a far larger and better equipped mobile Army than we have ever had before. Besides this, we have more than a million and a half men of the Home Guard, who are just as much soldiers of the Regular Army as the Grenadier Guards, and who are determined to fight for every inch of ground in every village and in every street.

Our fighting forces know that they have behind them a people who will not flinch or weary of the struggle – hard and protracted though it will be; but that we shall rather draw from the heart of suffering itself the means of inspiration and survival, and of a victory won not only for ourselves but for all. A victory won not only for our own time, but for the long and better days that are to come.

# POSTSCRIPT

*On 15 September there occurred what must have seemed like a remarkable echo for the many people to whom Charles Gardner's radio broadcast had heralded the beginning of the Battle of Britain. For on that later Sunday evening, the BBC again transmitted another eye-witness commentary by one of its broadcasters, Edward Ward, about the aerial battles which he had watched taking place in the skies over London. At the end of his graphic account, interspersed with the sound of gunfire, Ward broadcast a conversation he had had with a group of people who had actually been close to a German bomber which had crashed.*

*The people were clutching a number of souvenirs they had surreptitiously removed from the wreckage. One man was even carrying a single black leather airman's boot, which Ward described to his listeners. Through the middle of the boot, the broadcaster said, was a neat bullet-hole.*

*This time, when the report was broadcast there was no controversy about it – even its ghoulish finale. No protests to the BBC. No letters to* The Times. *It was clear now that listeners everywhere – thanks to the boys of Fighter Command – could 'take it' in every respect.*

*Londoners celebrate another day of victory in the skies – amidst the chaos on the ground!*

# ACKNOWLEDGEMENTS

I would like to record here my gratitude to a number of people and organisations for their help in the writing of this book. Many of my personal sources of information are named in the text, but I also wish to particularly thank W.O.G. Lofts, Angus Calder, Norman Longmate, Gavin Lyall, Ivor Halstead, Douglas Fairbanks jnr, Naomi Royde Smith, Basil Collier, Anthony Cardwell, Charles Merritt, Linda Stratford, Joan Cook, Virginia Cowles, John Moran, Leslie Broughton, Arthur Gordon, Edward Doran, and the late J.B. Priestley and Lord Dowding, all of whom assisted in my research in different but invaluable ways.

Among the organisations to whom I am also indebted are the Imperial War Museum, the RAF Archives, Hansard, the British Film Institute, BBC Sound Archives, the British Museum, the Newspaper Library at Colindale, the London Library, and the publishers, Jonathan Cape and Methuen Ltd.

The following publications have kindly allowed me to quote from their pages: *The Times, Daily Express, Daily Telegraph, Daily Mirror, Daily Mail, The Listener,* the *Illustrated London News, Picture Post, The Sphere, News Chronicle, The Sunday Times, Punch, London Mercury, The Spectator, The Guardian* and the *New York Times*.

A number of the photographs used in this book are from my own collection or have been loaned by friends and contributors, but copyright material has been supplied by the Air Ministry, the Imperial War Museum, Popperfoto, Keystone Press, The Photo Source, the Illustrated London News Picture Library and the Radio Times–Hulton Picture Library.

My admiration also goes to those who fought the Battle of Britain in the skies and on the ground of this redoubtable little island. We who mark the anniversary fifty years later owe them a debt we can never repay – only remember with gratitude.

Peter Haining

THE
SPITFIRE SUMMER

The people's-eye view of
the Battle of Britain

Wick

Turnhouse

**13 GROUP**

Acklington

Usworth

Aldergrove

Catterick

Church Fenton

Kirton-in-Lindsey

**12 GROUP**

Digby

E N G L A N D

Wittering        Coltishall

Pembrey

Duxford

Debden

**11 GROUP**

Filton

North Weald

**10 GROUP**

Northolt        Hornchurch

Middle Wallop

Kenley

St Eval

Biggin Hill        Ghen

Tangmere

Calais

*ENGLISH CHANNEL*

Cherbourg

Beauvais

Deauville        St. Cloud

Brest

3        PARIS

Dinard        Sèvres

Villacoublay

0        50        100

Miles

F R A N C E